The Official Biography of **John Chatham**

'Mr Big Healey'

Norman Burr : Foreword by Simon Taylor

Also from Veloce –

Biographies
André Lefebvre, and the cars he created at Voisin and Citroën (Beck)
Cliff Allison, The Official Biography of – From the Fells to Ferrari – (Gauld)
Edward Turner: The Man Behind the Motorcycles (Clew)
Jack Sears, The Official Biography of – Gentleman Jack (Gauld)
Jim Redman – 6 Times World Motorcycle Champion: The Autobiography (Redman)
Pat Moss Carlsson Story, The – Harnessing Horsepower (Turner)
Virgil Exner – Visioneer: The Official Biography of Virgil M Exner Designer Extraordinaire (Grist)

Rally Giants Series
Austin-Healey 100-6 & 3000 (Robson)

From Veloce Publishing's new imprints:

Soviet General & field rank officer uniforms: 1955 to 1991 (Streather)
Soviet military and paramilitary services: female uniforms 1941-1991 (Streather)

Hubble & Hattie

Complete Dog Manual, The – Gentle Dog Care (Robertson)
Dinner with Rover – delicious, nutritious meals for you and your dog to share (Paton-Ayre)
Dog Games – stimulating play to entertain your dog and you (Blenski)
Dog Relax – relaxed dogs, relaxed owners (Pilguj)
Know Your Dog – The guide to a beautiful relationship (Birmelin)
My dog is blind – but lives life to the full! (Horsky)
Smellorama! – nose games for dogs (Theby)
Waggy Tails & Wheelchairs (Epp)
Winston ... the dog who changed my life (Klute)
You and Your Border Terrier – The Essential Guide (Alderton)
You and Your Cockapoo – The Essential Guide (Alderton)

WWW.VELOCE.CO.UK

First published in April 2010 by Veloce Publishing Limited, Veloce House, Parkway Farm Business Park, Middle Farm Way, Poundbury, Dorchester, Dorset, DT1 3AR, England. Fax 01305 250479/e-mail info@veloce.co.uk/web www.veloce.co.uk or www.velocebooks.com.

Publishers Rod Grainger and Jude Brooks regard this book as a tribute to their mutual friend, Mike Kean: a true gentleman and a Big Healey fan of the first order. He is sadly missed by all who knew him.

ISBN: 978-1-845842-57-4 / UPC: 6-36847-04257-8

British Library Cataloguing in Publication Data – A catalogue record for this book is available from the British Library. Typesetting, design and page make-up all by Veloce Publishing Ltd on Apple Mac. Printed in India by Replika Press.

The Official Biography
of **John Chatham**

'Mr Big Healey'

VELOCE PUBLISHING
THE PUBLISHER OF FINE AUTOMOTIVE BOOKS

CONTENTS

DEDICATION
To Vicky,
for being a charming hostess to me and a wonderful wife to John.

FOREWORD BY SIMON TAYLOR

John Chatham represents a dying breed: not only in motor racing – into which, as this book demonstrates, he has channelled so much of his energy and determination to enjoy himself – but also in modern everyday life. In these days of 'elf 'n' safety' and the dreaded political correctness, many would see John as an anachronism. If that's what he is, he is proud of it.

Today, motor racing is a strictly commercial business. Even at its junior levels there are freshly-laundered overalls, gleaming motorhomes, silver-tongued PRs (public relations) and squeaky-clean drivers who can recite a sponsor's marketing strategy, but aren't allowed to have a sense of humour. John belongs to an earlier generation, one which regarded motorsport as fun, and not to be taken too seriously. It was a game to be played to the limit, after which friends and foes repaired to the pub to replay each move over another pint, and next day set about repairing the damage. To quote the T-shirt, John remembers the days when motor racing was dangerous, and sex was safe.

John and I have been friends for nearly half a century. We first met when I was a teenage cub reporter on the *Bristol Evening Post* in 1963, scurrying around that great city in search of news stories. One day my Austin A35 van was carrying me along the A38 when, on a crowded and somewhat disorganised forecourt at the junction with Egerton Road, I spied a red Austin-Healey 100, registered SAL 75. Deadlines forgotten, I stopped to admire it, and was immediately accosted by a character with a mischievous grin who, within moments, was trying to sell me the Healey. This was John, going through one of his periodic efforts to trade up in Healey terms. He sought to persuade me that the car was immaculate, and never raced or rallied, but I'd already remembered seeing it in tyre-torturing, valve-bouncing action in a local sprint. Realising that I was one jump ahead on that score, John immediately switched his sales patter to SAL's performance, and how it could eat 3000s for breakfast. In any case, I couldn't afford his asking price of £450, but that failed sale was the start of a friendship that endured throughout John's remarkable racing career, and endures today.

As a race reporter on *Autosport* I must have covered scores of John's races, in the UK and abroad, and I also carried out a track test of DD 300 during its wide-tyred Modsports period. John let me loose in it at Castle Combe – where else – and the car probably knew its way around without any input from me. But the experience still left me with renewed respect for John's ability, and his biceps.

Down the years John's stories, particularly when he has a glass in his hand, seem to have got ever more outrageous and far-fetched. Yet I have to tell you that, amazingly, pretty much all of them are true – pretty much. We're fortunate that Norman Burr has managed to unravel them all and get them written down, so that we can enjoy them again. But, as you read this book, make sure you have a glass in your hand. It's more fun that way.

PREFACE & ACKNOWLEDGEMENTS

There is no trophy cabinet in John Chatham's house. He has never kept a diary and his photo collection, though considerable, consists of a large drawer bulging with unlabelled prints.

Anyone who knows 'Chat,' as he is called by his family and friends, will not be surprised by this, for John has always competed for enjoyment and lived for the moment. But it does present a considerable challenge to his biographer. How do you reconstruct the career of a driver who raced, rallied, sprinted, trialled and hillclimbed for 40 years all over Britain and the Continent, in hundreds – probably thousands – of events, run by dozens of organizations, some of which are defunct and most of which have never digitized their records? John has an excellent memory, but even the brightest grey cells are dimmed by time.

The solution – and I apologize right now to anyone who is disappointed by this – is not to try. Although Appendix 2 at the back of this book summarizes the things he remembers most – good and bad – about his sporting career, if you are seeking to find out how many sprints he won in 1963 you will be disappointed. I do not pretend the information is complete, but it is to the best of my knowledge accurate.

In fact, that comment also applies to the book as a whole. This is not a scholarly tome, but John Chatham's life as John Chatham remembers it, fleshed out with recollections from family and friends, but otherwise unembellished. Its priorities are his priorities – cars and people, events and incidents, not silverware and statistics.

Over the years, journalists have used lots of adjectives to describe John. Hairy, genial, bespectacled, burly, wild and woolly, wily, mischievous and Falstaffian are just a few. Those closer to him know him as an unreconstructed maverick with a single-minded determination to do his own thing, right or wrong, sensible or otherwise, showing scant regard for the rulebook or, sometimes, for the people around him.

Yet despite this, he has inspired unswerving loyalty and affection from friends, customers, employees and – most of all – from his wife Vicky. While researching this book I've been struck again and again by how many of his friends in Bristol and around the world are still involved with Big Healeys, how many of the friendships go back decades, and how everyone seems to work for everyone else.

Up to a point of course, there is nothing unusual in this – many friendships are born out of mutual enthusiasm and in time the social contact often comes to mean much more than the original interest. But John Chatham has become the hub of his own little universe, and the gravitational pull keeping it all together is his natural good humour, plus a dab of showmanship and a large dollop of sheer 'brass neck.' You may not always approve of what he does, but you'd have to be a very miserable character indeed not to admire his style – and the fact that he gets away with it so often. John often comments that he seems to have lived a charmed life and maybe those around him subconsciously hope that the good fortune will somehow rub off on them. He's often stubborn and sometimes downright infuriating, but there is no malice in the man and no one ever accused him of being dull. People just can't help liking him.

Most of this I have learned during the past two years,

for although I came across John a number of times during my student days in Bristol (1967-73), we were never more than acquaintances. When I approached him in 2007 with the idea of writing his biography, I knew only a modest amount about him and he knew virtually nothing about me. Indeed he had to wrack his brains to remember me at all. So the 24 months we have worked together on his biography have been a voyage of discovery for me, as much as a voyage of rediscovery for him.

I hope you enjoy the book as much as we have enjoyed the journey. It's been great fun, and Courage's Best Bitter has never tasted so good.

Norman Burr
Lancaster, England

❧

ACKNOWLEDGEMENTS

Clearly, the biggest thank you must go to John Chatham himself, who spent many hours talking into my tape recorder, not to mention quite a few more in the pub, in order to provide the material for this book. But hot on his heels must be Vicky Chatham: not only was her own contribution invaluable, her impeccable hospitality made me feel more like an old friend than an incomer.

A long list of other people have contributed reminiscences, research and photos, and I am grateful to all of them – in alphabetical order they include Tony Barron, Steve Bicknell, Alain de Cadenet, Joe Chatham, Sandra Coombe, Phil Coombs, Joe Cox, Peter Dzwig, Art Eastman, Pete Farmer, Mary Harvey, George Holt, John Horne, Nick Howell, Mike Jiggle, Kaye Kovacs, Henri and Béatrice Maisonneuve, Christine Maxwell, Steve Norton, Colin Pearcy, Dan Pendergraft, D Randy Riggs, Phil Saddington, Sandie Savory, Kaage Schildt, Mark Schmidt, Jack Sears, Ian Shapland, John Simcock, Doug Smith, Al Stacey, Simon Taylor, Willie Tuckett, Ted Walker, Ted Williams, Ted Worswick and Philip Young. And last but not least, the archive departments of Autosport and Motor Sport magazines.

Particular thanks go to Joe Cox. As a former garage manager at Egerton Road and long-term competition manager of the Austin-Healey Club, Joe is uniquely well informed. He was instrumental in getting this biography off the ground initially and has proved to be a vital source of motorsport information as well as a tireless researcher.

I would also like to thank my own family and friends for their tolerance and encouragement – particularly Al Stacey, who gave me the idea in the first place.

And we must not forget Jim Watson, whose inimitable cartoons have illuminated some of the moments the camera was not around to record.

All photos are from the personal collection of John Chatham except where otherwise marked. The author has made every reasonable effort to contact the copyright holder in every case where he believes permission to be required, but in some cases, particularly with older photographs, it has not been possible to locate the party concerned. The author would be obliged if those parties, or their agents or heirs, would contact him at the address below:

Norman Burr, 5 Laurel Bank, Lancaster LA1 5LN, UK
Tel: +44 (0)1524 849079
Mobile: +44 (0)7729 618861
Email: nburr@talktalk.net

ABOUT THE AUTHOR

Originally trained as an engineer at Rolls-Royce Aero Engines and Bath University, lifelong petrolhead Norman Burr has been a technical journalist practically all his working life, firstly with professional and industrial magazines, then as a freelance and subsequently through Pagefast Ltd, a small printing and publishing company which he helped found. In 2006, wanting to get off the production treadmill and give himself scope for projects like this, he left the company and reverted to freelance work. Most of his output concerns sport aviation and automotive subjects.

Mr Big Healey is the fourth book he has written and the sixth with which he has been involved. It is his first fully-fledged biography.

By the same author:
• *Ultralight & Microlight Aircraft of the World*, co-written with Alain-Yves Berger, published 1983 (also published in French as Tous les ULM du Monde).
• *Ultralight & Microlight Aircraft of the World Second Edition*, co-written with Alain-Yves Berger, published 1985.
• *Living with Speed*, a partly biographical look at the speed hillclimb scene through the eyes of Roy Lane's 1996 season, published 1997.

Contributed to:
• *32 Days to Beijing*, travelogue by James Edmonds about a microlight flight from London to China, published 1994.
• *Gertie's Day Out*, travelogue by Eve Jackson about emigrating to Tanzania by microlight, published 2006.

The author with 661 CGT.

YOUTHFUL INSPIRATION

No matter how much thought we put into the major decisions of our lives, fate will insist on playing its part. The most trivial decision can turn out to have dramatic and completely unforeseeable results. The young John Chatham was no exception: his future hung on his father's desire for a 'fag' (cigarette).

It was wartime, 25 September 1940 to be exact, and Chief Engineer Joe Chatham was at work in the Bristol Aeroplane Company at Filton, where he had been seconded from Birmingham in 1938 to work on aero engines as part of the rearmament drive. Some five miles (8km) away in Downend, his wife Elsie was in the garden chatting to the neighbours, her six-month old son in her arms. She heard the rumble of aircraft engines – nothing unusual over this air-minded city – and watched with pride as over 50 bombers appeared on the horizon. But then the air raid siren went and her pride turned to horror, as she realized they were not British planes. The daylight raid on Bristol and its aircraft factories had begun. As the bombs started to fall "she dived into a cabbage patch with me in her arms," John relates.

Meanwhile, at the factory, everyone scrambled to the shelters. Everyone that is, except Joe. Like practically everybody in those days, he smoked, and right now he fancied a surreptitious 'ciggy.' So instead of heading for the shelter he dived into a nearby pillbox, manned by a guard whom he knew. The shelter he should have gone into suffered a direct hit and everyone inside was killed. The same blast lifted Joe's pillbox bodily and turned it round to face another direction, but the occupants survived.

Had Joe followed the rules, his infant son would have

John as a baby.

had no dad and young John's life would have been very different. The family would not have bought a garage after the war and John would not have been exposed to the influences that turned him into a lifelong enthusiast for cars in general and Austin-Healeys in particular. But Joe went his own way and, as it happened, everyone benefited, with the possible exception of the Nazi war effort. It was a lesson in independent thinking that would not be lost on his son in the years ahead. However, we are getting ahead of ourselves.

The Chathams were Brummies. The first Chatham to find his way into the history books was John's great great grandfather, Waterloo Bob. As his family moniker suggests, he was one of the lucky few who returned from the battle that finally destroyed Napoleon's empire. Bob was quite a celebrity at the time – "apparently when he died there were about 1000 people at his funeral," John explains. But this military fame was something of a one-off: the Chathams were a typical Birmingham family, more into making things than blowing them up, and father Joe was an engineer from a long line of engineers and craftsmen.

"They were all very hands-on. Father was one of thirteen, and mother one of nine, though not all survived to adulthood. One of my father's brothers was a great furniture maker and one of his sisters was quite an artist; she did a complete family-tree book, which my sister Pamela still has. My father used to go up and down to Birmingham and I used to go with him, I remember my grandparents house, his family were quite artistic."

These trips to Birmingham were not frequent, however. The move to Bristol had isolated Joe and Elsie, and John reckons he probably has cousins, aunts and uncles he has never met, plus others he's seen only at weddings and funerals. The Midlands became a memory as Downend and Filton became the centres of his parents' wartime world, Joe often walking the whole 5 miles (8km) to work, through blacked-out streets.

Joe's career in the aircraft industry was no accident. Aircraft were his passion. He wanted to fly and volunteered to join the RAF at the outbreak of war, but the authorities decided he was much more useful where he was. "You're needed to make the planes fly," was the blunt response. He was not to be denied entirely, however. Desperate to get into the air, he spent any spare time he could find at weekends down at Castle Combe, later to be a racing circuit, but at that time used for pilot training. There he would teach young pilots to fly. "So at least he kept his hand in and enjoyed a little bit of flying. Later in life," John continues with a mischievous and somewhat admiring grin, "he always fantasized that he was a great Spitfire pilot, but he wasn't really."

John, born on 3 March 1940, was only five when the war ended and recalls only disconnected incidents from those years. "People rushing out with a bucket and shovel after a horse had gone by – to take the manure for their garden. Walking down to the village shops with mum – apparently one day a bus pulled up at the stop and I said, 'mummy, mummy, engine, engine,' so even then it seems I had an eye and an ear for motors. And I can vaguely remember the Anderson air-raid shelter we had in the garden, it was semi-underground."

One reason he remembers the shelter is that he spent a lot of time playing in it with Philip Parkinson, who lived a few doors away. Philip, these days the proud owner of a 550 Maranello, has stayed in contact with his childhood chum and now divides his time between Spain and Portishead. Much later he would inadvertently play a vital role in John's life, introducing him to the woman who has run his administrative affairs for over 20 years.

John's other playmate was Peter Long, who lived next door. "Peter and I used to go and hide, and one night, when it was getting dark, my parents couldn't find us anywhere. We weren't in the shelter, we weren't in the garden, and we weren't in the street. They got really worried, went round all the neighbours, no one had seen us. They were all gathered together, ready to start combing the area, when they found us, sitting there happily in the chicken shed, with chicken shit everywhere. We stank like hell, but we wouldn't come out."

Not long after this, in 1946, John acquired a baby sister, Pamela. The big age gap, plus the fact that she didn't seem interested in cars or in getting dirty, meant that, "we were never on the same wavelength," in John's words. They still live within a few miles of each other and get along well enough on the rare occasions when they meet, but right from childhood they have gone their separate ways.

Little girls, he decided, were dull. They weren't interested in cars, they weren't much good at games, they didn't even collect birds' eggs, unlike many lads at the time, John included. "I had a friend who used to love birds and he hated people who saved birds' eggs, so I couldn't tell him that I had a few in my little collection. We used to go down and spy on this moorhen's eggs; there was an island in the middle of the pond in the park and, if you climbed to the top of the slide, you could look down on the nest. We used to do it regularly to make sure the eggs were all there.

"One day I woke very early, went down the road, looked at the nest and thought, 'I'm going to get one of those eggs.' But I didn't want to get home all wet and bedraggled, so I took all my clothes off, waded out waist-high into this pond, had an egg away, got dressed and scuttled back home. Later on, the friend and I walked down to the park to check on the eggs. 'Bugger me,' he said, 'somebody's had one of those.' I never did tell him who it was."

John was always game for a challenge. "One day when I was nine years old I invented a game with my mates. The idea was to see how fast we could run up the steps of the slide, slide down and run back round to the steps. We'd do that four times on the trot and time ourselves. I wanted to be the fastest of course, and I found it was

Egerton Road garage in 1949, pretty much as Joe and Elsie bought it three years later.

quicker to run up the steps, jump off the top, and land on the slide halfway down. But on one occasion I missed the slide and went straight over the top, thumped to the ground and broke my arm."

It was a painful lesson, but it did nothing to stem his competitiveness. Just once, when John was 10 or 11, Joe took him to a football match in Downend, but in truth John was too much of an individualist to be inspired by team sports. His will to win came out in other ways. He had the habit of saying to his mates, "why don't we try this ..." and his mates, often against their better judgement, would think, "why not?"

By now he'd left Christ Church Junior School in Downend and moved to Staple Hill Secondary Modern. "There was a winding road from the school to the main road," John recalls, "and we used to race to see who could pedal to the main road first. I had to be the fastest." Inspired by the occasional evening at Bristol Speedway with his dad, he had no qualms about exploring the limits on two wheels.

Other than speedway, however, suburban Bristol in the early '50s didn't provide much stimulation for a motor-minded kid. Cars were mostly old, or black, or smoky, and often all three. Commercial vehicles could be much

more interesting. John remembers what must have been one of the last commercial uses of steam wagons, Foden steamers delivering beer to the pub on the corner, just 40 yards from his house.

However, that stimulation was about to be provided, in spades, because Joe and Elsie had decided to go into business. In peacetime, the aircraft industry was contracting and Joe finally decided that his future lay elsewhere. In 1952, the couple took the plunge and bought Egerton Road Garage in Bishopston, on the corner of Egerton Road and the main A38 Gloucester Road. The family moved from Downend to the house that came with the garage, choosing literally and metaphorically to live with the business. They were risking everything: if the venture didn't succeed, there was more than just a job at stake.

As the removal van drove away, bill paid, job done, Joe was left with just 17 shillings and sixpence in his pocket and a family of four to support. There was no money in the bank to fund the purchase of the first tanker-load of petrol, which, even in those days, was bought by direct debit. So there was nothing for it but to go cap in hand to Esso and ask for special treatment. A deal was done: Egerton Road Garage was in business.

It was tough going and needed total commitment from both of them to make a go of it. Joe fixed the cars, Elsie handled the paperwork. 'Handled' is perhaps an understatement, as Elsie rapidly became a force to be reckoned with. Any 'difficult' customer was liable to find Elsie, spanner in hand and rapping the desk like an auctioneer on heat, standing between him and the exit and announcing at the rate of one rap per word that, "you're-not-leaving-this-garage-till-you've-paid-your-bill." Only the foolhardy or the seriously broke ran that particular gauntlet. "She was quite a religious woman," recalls John, "a regular churchgoer, sang in the church choir, made us go to Sunday school every week and signed the pledge. That's why I'm such a good boy today," he grins.

Joe, however, engineered a little leeway for himself. Even though alcohol was not encouraged in the house, he sneaked the occasional tipple from a bottle of scotch tucked away in the stores. He never talked much to John about his youth, but a story he told much later, after he took up model-making in his retirement, hints at a wilder side to his character.

"Come and look at this," he'd said to John, showing him a model he'd just finished of a horse-drawn brewer's dray. Incongruously, the van had seat belts for the driver and his mate. "You think seat belts are a modern idea, came out on cars in the 1950s? Not a bit of it."

Apparently, in his youth in the '20s Joe had been a drayman's mate on just such a vehicle. Even in those days most businesses had gone over to motors, but the breweries, being very traditional, stuck to horses long after everyone else. Joe and his driver toured the pubs everyday, delivering beer, and at every pub they were given a free pint. "By the end of the day we were pissed as a fart and kept rolling off," Joe laughed. "The horse knew where we were going, we didn't!" So many drivers fell off, some of them even getting run over by their own cart, that the brewery, with commendable practicality, fitted the drays with belts.

As far as John is concerned, however, life began in 1952. He was 12 years of age, he'd just started at a new school (Bishop Road) and his family had just moved to the garage in Bishopston. Cars came and went, for repairs, servicing, and petrol. A few were new, some were tidy, most had seen better days, but almost all were dull, black, sidevalve and square. Then one day an Austin-Healey 100 appeared in the window of Henly's, the Austin main dealer in Bristol, not half a mile down the Gloucester Road from the family garage.

John couldn't take his eyes off it. Low, curvaceous and bright red, this apparition revolving on a plinth in the window transfixed the impressionable 12-year-old. Night

12-year-old John just after moving to Egerton Road, with dad's 2¹/₂-litre Jaguar, which he owned for several years before replacing it with a Vauxhall Velox.

"... this apparition revolving on a plinth in the window transfixed the impressionable 12-year-old." (© Jim Watson)

after night he cycled down the Gloucester Road to burn his nose on the window and gaze longingly at it for hour after hour. At a stroke, it made the dismal black boxes grinding up the hill to Filton look little better than billy carts. Here was colour, power, speed and excitement! Away with austerity, this was living! There and then, he made up his mind to own one.

So big an impression did that red Healey make that John related this story 25 years later, at a commemorative dinner chaired by legendary '50s motorsport commentator Raymond Baxter. A 'Healey hundred' had gathered to celebrate the Healey 100's 25th anniversary, one hundred people arranged in ten tables of ten. After dinner, Baxter worked his way round each table in turn, picking out one person to tell their favourite Healey anecdote. John, sitting on the Austin-Healey Club table, expected the club chairman to be asked to speak, but instead Baxter put him on the spot.

"If I'd had time to think about it, maybe I'd have had said something sensible, but I hadn't, so I didn't. I said the first thing that came into my head, about this beautiful curvaceous body that was circulating in the window of Henly's in Gloucester Road, with me, a young boy, peering in. I told them that was where I experienced my first orgasm, and only later in life did I learn that there were other curvaceous bodies, which could have a similar effect. That went down with quite a roar. It wasn't far from the truth either."

With his parents working flat out at the garage, with the best will in the world there was never going to be much time to sit down with the kids and help with their homework. John and Pamela were left largely to their own devices and John admits that it wasn't very good for him. "I was always up to something or other, always a complete rebel. I didn't like many lessons and if I didn't like something, I didn't do it.

"But I did quite lean to metalwork and woodwork, where for a while I was the golden boy, the teacher's pet. I did everything so well I was put forward as an example. But that didn't last long because at the beginning of one term the teacher told each of us to choose a project, something that would take all term to do. As I was pretty proficient, the teacher suggested I tackle something difficult, to occupy more of my time, so we agreed I'd make a table.

"So I made a table. Trouble was, I made it in just half a term. The teacher didn't give me anything else to do, so I spent the rest of the term making really sharp darts and throwing them round the classroom. By the end of term I wasn't the golden boy any more!" (That honour undoubtedly goes to Bishop Road's most famous pupil, Cary Grant, who is commemorated by a plaque at the school).

It would be another year before John had his first hands-on contact with a Healey. "Late in '53 we had a customer with a green BN1," he recalls. This gloriously low, svelte machine seemed like an unattainable dream, but nevertheless he decided it was time to start earning some money.

Joe checking the tyres of a customer's MkI Zodiac in 1956.

"Dad employed a Scotsman called, inevitably, Jock. On Saturdays I used to help him and father, cleaning cars and the like. Jock, incidentally, is the reason why even now I talk about, 'wee this,' and, 'wee that,' I was brought up with him and the word has stuck.

"In a full Saturday I could wash up to 13 cars at 5 shillings a time. Back in 1954 that was good money and I prided myself on being the richest guy at school. Then I went one better. A retired colonel came in driving a big old Lanchester and said, 'I want you to wash my Lanchester and my Austin Seven. As it's two cars, I'm going to pay you 7 shillings and sixpence for the pair. And I don't want them done here, I want you to cycle to my house.' So after I'd washed all the cars at the garage, I'd cycle to Filton, at the back of the aerodrome, to wash another two. As a result, I'd have a fiver in my pocket, or at least a couple of pound notes, when all the other kids had pennies. I didn't mind hard graft, as long as I saw a return for my efforts.

"Of course, at that time I was still too young to drive legally. But although I was just a little schoolboy and was not supposed to be driving, I could not stay away from cars, so I used to make a nuisance of myself by jumping into cars on the garage forecourt. Then one day I went a stage further. Father had a row of lock-up garages and inside one of them was a Vauxhall Velox (like my father's) belonging to an old gentleman, who I knew was in hospital. So I thought, 'he won't know, he won't mind, if I just have a little go in his car.'

"A Bank Holiday weekend was approaching and my parents were going away. They wanted me to go with them. I planned on not going because I planned on driving this car. And I did. I drove it about six miles down to the River Severn, then drove it back. Naturally I was curious to know how quickly it went and how it went round corners and then, being a bit exuberant, I overcooked it and hit the bank. There was no damage to the exterior of the car, but it put a lot of grass between the tyre and the wheel. Then, to round the trip off, on the way home it ran out of petrol on a hill. I didn't really look old enough to be driving this car, so I didn't fancy drawing attention to myself by pushing it into a filling station, especially with mud and grass adorning it. Fortunately I found a gallon of petrol in the boot, put that in and drove it back. Then I spent hours trying to remove the muck with a penknife, so nobody ever knew I'd actually borrowed the car."

Emboldened, he got behind the wheel whenever he could. "The garage had a contract to service the vans of a local bakery. Because their premises were nearby, the vans were stored at the bakery and the keys left with us to collect whichever vehicle was due for service that week. The temptation there was to wait until late in the evening when they'd all closed up, pick up a van, drive it down Gloucester Road and round Bristol city centre, then put it back safely without anyone knowing. That was rather more daring, because there were always police officers around in the city centre. I did this for sometime; I never damaged any of the vans and nobody ever knew."

By now John was 15 and eager to leave Bishop Road School. Academia held no attraction for him, he wanted to work with cars. "I bumbled around for a time in the garage until my father decided that I needed to get out and do a proper apprenticeship. As he knew the MD (Managing Director) of the local Rootes Group agent, he got me a job – in their commercial department because that was more hands-on – and I started my engineering apprenticeship, at Cathedral Garage.

"It was a bit rocky going because I wasn't the easiest kid to deal with, I was full of scams, jokes and tricks. The first day I was there I was found pumping grease out of the grease gun onto the floor and then wiping it round the joints to make it look like I'd greased them. I was dealt with quite severely, dunked in a 50 gallon drum full of sawdust and rammed in so hard that I almost choked, but I survived.

"I got very upset with the other lads for playing tricks on me, even though in reality they were only giving as good as they'd already got. Nevertheless, one day I decided

"... being a bit exuberant, I overcooked it and hit the bank." (© Jim Watson)

"... somebody touched the bench and all hell let loose."
(© Jim Watson)

another one was due. We had a cage where the guys used to do their bench work, and the benches in there were all-steel. While they were off at lunch I wired this bench to the mains, to teach them a lesson." In a masterpiece of understatement John adds: "It wasn't very sensible really, but at 15, who cares?"

Needless to say, when the other apprentices came back from lunch, somebody touched the bench and all hell let loose. "They couldn't find out who did it, but they all put the blame on me, I don't remember why. I was always the one in trouble."

Transport, officially at least, was still a humble push-bike, but John did his best to make the most of it. "It was a slight downhill most of the way from my father's garage on Gloucester Road to Cathedral Garage in the city centre, so I used to pedal like fury and see how many cars I could overtake. One morning, going through the traffic lights at the end of Gloucester Road, where the road curves slightly, I was going so fast that I lost it completely and there's me on this bike, sliding around in the middle of the crossroads with cars everywhere." His guardian angel was obviously on duty that day.

Eventually, the magic age of 17 was reached and John could get himself a driving licence. "The first vehicle I got to use regularly was an old Willys Jeep that we had lying around the garage. This was 1957, the days of fuel shortages following the Suez Crisis, and the law had been amended to allow learner drivers to drive unaccompanied, which was great. I used to take the boys from work down the road and frighten them by seeing how fast I could go between the lampposts and the wall with about half an

inch to spare – lunatic! That Jeep didn't last too long and finally died on me.

"After that father let me drive his Vauxhall Velox. It was an L Series, similar to the one I'd sneaked my first drive in, and I eventually took my test in it. But as I didn't have to have a driver with me, I didn't give a shit whether I passed or not. In fact I failed miserably and the examiner filled out a full foolscap sheet with complaints about my driving."

Later that year the law reverted to normal and John needed to pass a test if he was to continue to drive unaccompanied. Moreover, the situation had suddenly become urgent, as testosterone had belatedly entered the frame. Not until he was 17 did he have eyes for any curve other than the flank of a Healey, but in 1957, the year of Paul Anka's worldwide hit *Diana*, John developed a crush on a girl of the same name in the local pub. "I thought she was wonderful," he recalls fondly. It came to nothing, but his priorities would never be so unidirectional again.

"Father said that if I did pass the test I could use his car to go on holiday, and I'd decided to go to Butlins holiday camp where there were known to be lots of young ladies. It was most important that I pass, so I had a local police instructor teach me how to drive correctly. On the completion of the second test I said, 'what did I fail on?' and the examiner said he'd never come across a young guy so confident and disinclined to make mistakes. I told him it was down to the fact that this time it mattered, last time it didn't." Cheekily, John added: "And anyway, I didn't like the look of the first examiner, but I liked the look of you, so I did it properly."

Armed with a licence, he bought his first car, a MkII Ford Consul convertible with a Raymond Mays conversion. It was no Healey, but it was a handsome car in its day and with the Mays head offered respectable performance. John thought it was the bee's knees. Moreover, thanks to the bench seat and column change, "there was nothing in the way, you could have a good snog while you were driving." He speaks from experience as he had his first serious girlfriend, Jackie, around this time.

John stayed at Cathedral Garage for three years, but the writing was on the wall. "After my little misdemeanours I wasn't the best loved guy," he admits. "Eventually, one Friday afternoon, the foreman gave me 48 hours to buck up my ideas. I thought, 'that doesn't sound too hard, I'm not here for 48 hours!' but in fact that wasn't quite true because in those days you worked Saturday morning. So I kept my nose clean on Saturday morning, and for the rest of the 48 hours, but on Monday morning I came to a decision. My mother had gone into hospital, so my father was busier than ever. I told him my apprenticeship might be terminated because of my behaviour, so I might

Hanging out with the lads in a friend's garage at around the age of 18. Left to right: a mate from Egerton Road, schoolmate John Gow, and John; others unknown.

Joe and Elsie with John's sister Pamela in the early 1960s.

as well hand in my notice and come and work for him. I don't quite know what he thought, but I'm sure he was glad of the help."

Despite enjoying the Consul, it wasn't long before it didn't feel fast enough. A six-cylinder Zephyr convertible seemed the answer, not least because it had a woman-pulling power hood whereas the Consul's was manual. Joe, however, must have had misgivings, because one day, out of the blue, he said to John, "Isn't it about time you bought yourself a decent car?"

"He'd nothing against Zephyrs," John explains, "but maybe he thought mine was dangerous because the top came off, and he thought it too powerful for a young lunatic like me. He wasn't interested in speed, he always said, 'size and speed cost money,' and of course he was right."

Joe had no interest in motorsport, regarding it as an expensive folly. Apart from a trip to the 1938 British GP (Grand Prix) at Donington, and those occasional evenings at Bristol Speedway when John was a lad, Joe had never attended a motorsport event in his entire life. But ironically, his suggestion proved to be the starting point of his son's motorsport career, the green light John had been subconsciously waiting for.

As instructed, he looked around for a 'decent car' and identified two. "Funnily enough, they were both Healey 100s, not at all what my father had in mind! One was a beautiful black BN2, at £515 far above my price bracket. The other was a rebuilt damaged car, a BN1, price £365 – I bought it."

John had his first Healey, and a red one at that.

Exploring the curves

2

It was 1960, and the 20-year-old Chatham, young, fit and confident, wanted an outlet for his competitive instincts. SAL 75, his newly acquired red Healey 100, needed to be stretched – as did he.

At this time a national Austin-Healey Club was still in the process of being formed, so John had to look elsewhere for a sporting outlet. "I wanted a competition licence, so I had to be a member of an RAC (Royal Automobile Club) affiliated club. I joined the White Horse Motor Club, a little club based in Bristol, where I soon met this guy with a Healey 100, called Frank Walker. I mentioned the new Healey club and the two of us went to the inaugural meeting of the South Western Centre. I was on the committee on day one and that's when I started in motorsport."

The Austin-Healey Club was started by BMC (British Motor Corporation) in 1961, by encouraging existing Healey-oriented clubs to band together under a national umbrella. The membership of the Healey Drivers Club, which had hitherto concentrated on earlier Healeys like Abbotts and Silverstones, transferred to the Midland Centre, while the Southern Counties Sprite Club became the Southern Counties Centre. Sprite clubs in the north and east took on parallel roles.

By contrast, the South Western (SW) Centre was starting from scratch, though its Bristol base did attract a number of the more westerly Southern Counties Sprite owners. To help it on its way, Peter Browning, who worked for BMC at Abingdon and had been heavily involved in setting up the national club, took the trouble to drive down to Bristol for the inaugural meeting. He brought with him Alan Zafer, the Abingdon PR man.

Leaping in at the start of a driving test in the early 1960s.

First ever speed event: 1960 at Church Lawford near Rugby, SAL 75 second in queue.

John with SAL 75, his first Healey, and fellow Healey owner Derek Park. The two were born only three weeks apart and this photo was taken when they were both 21. With his 21st birthday money Derek bought what became DP 1769, a yellow 3000 MkI with a Ruddspeed conversion and lots of other mods.

No one realized it at the time, but that gathering at a pub on the road to Weston-super-Mare was a seminal event. Many of the people in the room would go on to become lifelong friends and remain involved with Healeys for decades. Just two or three SW Centre meetings down the road, John's local network of Healey aficionados would be firmly in place, with names like Tony Sampson, Alan Harvey, Tony Fowles and John Bristow in his address book, and his social life would have a Healey-dominated focus, which it has never lost. "Eighteen of us from that inaugural meeting still get together every year," John adds with obvious pleasure, "including Alan Zafer, who I still see regularly."

But the driving force behind the SW Centre would not be John. That honour went to Frank Walker, "a bombastic fellow, a great character."

John continues: "He ran it like a regimental sergeant major and what he said, went. He ruled the roost – he had

a big whip. If he said, 'you've got to be outside my house at seven o'clock on Sunday morning, we're going to a sprint at Blackbushe,' or whatever, we'd all go along with it. We were just glad that things were happening. Even if it was a distance away, we were up for it: we didn't worry so much about drinking and driving in those days, we and the sergeant major did quite a lot of that on the way back. Fortunately, we all survived that era.

"Frank's way of doing things was rather good for the club at the start, but eventually the members couldn't put up with him any more. People got tired of being instructed to go and spend a whole day chasing round in a circle at some windy bloody airfield in the middle of the country. We still did those things of course, but we wanted a say about when and where."

The car which underpinned all this, SAL 75, "was bog standard when I got it," recalls John, but inevitably it didn't stay that way. "In those days it was easy to develop a car:

John (immediately to the right of the car) with an Austin 7 modded for driving tests at the White Horse Motor Club. The mod? The steering arm was reversed, so turning left made the car go right ...

half an inch more wheel width here, a few thou off the head there. But I didn't do anything radical to it, nor did most other owners. Just tinkered with this and tinkered with that." Subtle stuff, like experiments with spring and damper rates, and serious stuff, like special competition engines, belonged to the future.

A poor photo, but significant: John's only shot of SW Centre Sergeant Major Frank Walker, at the wheel of SAL 75 in a driving test in '62 or '63.

"At the time you could buy a Le Mans conversion to turn the BN1 into a 100M. I bought one of these kits from the Donald Healey Motor Company in Warwick; it consisted of two HS6 carbs to replace the HS4s, a different camshaft and a distributor with a better advance curve. It came in a kit with a cold-air box and the whole thing cost £33. You could get it fitted by the Donald Healey Motor Co, in fact towards the end of BN2 production you could order a factory-built 100M, the BN2N. The few that were factory-built also came with higher compression and a louvred bonnet made in steel. All later louvred bonnets were ally, so if you have a steel one it's original.

"My first serious mod was to fit this kit. But before long I did what all young boys do, I skimmed the head, to mimic the factory version. Straight off the production

SAL hard at work in September 1962 – approaching The Gate at Wiscombe Park Hillclimb ... (© Ted Walker)

line, a standard 100 was said to be 7.5:1 but the ones I've checked are only 7:1 – pretty low, but then this was a long-stroke pre-war design."

Of course, it wasn't long before tinkering turned to serious tuning and the head was off again, in search of more power. "This time I fitted different pistons, so that the compression crept up even higher, to around 10.5. And at 10.5, they break crankshafts, as I discovered to my cost! I was coming back from a sprint at Castle Combe one day, got as far as Muller Road in Bristol and the engine suddenly became rough and noisy. It just about got me home, where I found that the crank had broken across the web, it was only held together by the fracture. When I rebuilt it, I dropped the compression to 9:1, that's the most they will take reliably."

Nowadays many Healey 100s and 100Ms have alloy heads, but these were not available at the time. "They didn't come in until the 1990s," explains John, "although the 100S [a rare competition variant] used them in period as they give much better cooling and combustion. They are relatively easy to make with modern foundry techniques and alloys, but at first the FIA (Federation Internationale de l'Automobile) didn't like them and said alloy heads were non-original. However, the original iron heads are tending to fatigue now and the only replacements available are alloy, so I think they have had to soften their stance."

A popular modification was to replace the front drums with discs from a 3000. "You could buy all the bits new and it meant you could go that bit harder because

... and at Castle Combe that same month. (© Ted Walker)

you could stop that bit quicker." John also swapped the original three-speed box for a later four-speed, introduced on the BN2 version of the Healey 100, whilst retaining the overdrive.

This is not the place for a detailed history of the marque, but a bit of background from John will not go amiss at this point.

"Donald Healey, canny operator that he was, visited the Austin factory and saw this pile of bits left over from the Austin A90 Atlantic. They'd produced all these engines, four-speed gearboxes and back axles, but the cars fell flat on their face in the American market, they would not sell at all. Healey thought, 'if I put the 2.6 into a sports car I could use a lower-ratio axle and blank off first gear. Then provided I fit an overdrive to restore the overall gearing, I

could advertise the car in the US as having synchromesh on first gear.' In 1953 no other sports car had that."

Healey proceeded to design a chassis around this running gear, then clothed it in a pretty body and fitted a folding windscreen – "a clever idea, as with the screen down it looked like a rather smooth boulevard cruiser." The Austin management was impressed enough to sell him the parts at a good price provided he called the car Austin-Healey, and so a marque was born. Austin supplied the drivetrain, Jensen the body, and the Donald Healey Motor Co brought them together in prototype form at Warwick. The resulting package was put into production at the MG factory in Abingdon and is known in the Healey world as a BN1. It was a huge success, especially in the United States.

The 2.6 engine designed for the Atlantic was a derivative of the 2.2-litre A70 engine used in the Austin Hampshire and Hereford models (although the blocks were cast slightly differently, so you can't turn a 2.2 into a 2.6). The 2.6's internals were common to the six-cylinder 4-litre D Series, which is effectively one and a half Atlantic engines. This unit was used in the Sheerline and Princess models and saw service right into the 1960s, when the last Princesses left the line. It also, incidentally, found its way into Jensen's 541.

The first major change to the Austin-Healey 100 was the introduction of a stronger gearbox in 1955 for the BN2 model, with four usable ratios. The BN2 also boasted wider front drums. Not many were produced, however, as it was replaced only a year or so later by the first of the six-cylinder cars, the 100/6, which ran until 1959 when the Healey 3000 was introduced.

The arrival of the 100/6 ended the standard-fitment overdrive, though it was still available on option, and introduced a new option of two-plus-two seating, a choice which continued right through until the Healey 3000 MkII, which saw the pure two-seaters dropped early in its production run. These last few two-seaters are John's favourite Healey, boasting the oval grille and late-type centre-change gearbox, but unencumbered by luxury goodies. After this point the car moved upmarket, with all models having rear seats and the option of a more luxurious convertible body, with winding windows.

In the early 1960s, a Healey 100 was an entry ticket to all forms of motorsport. "In that one car I did production car trials, autocrosses, rallies, sprints, hillclimbs, race meetings, the lot. And it was competitive in all of them; I won awards at every level. It wasn't often quick enough to win outright, after all it wasn't a new car even then – my Healey 100 was

six years old and the design nearer eight – but you could have fun and you wouldn't disgrace yourself. The Healey 100 was a good all-rounder, lots of torque, and you could do quite a bit with the car to improve it. Mind you, it was the same car you went to work in on Monday morning, so you couldn't afford to bend it at the weekend."

A certain amount of bending was, of course, inevitable. Like all young drivers, John took a while to strike the right balance between bravado and self-preservation, and in the interim he had a few close shaves. "I remember one of the first sprints I entered; it was at Hullavington. On the very first bend, a left-hander, I drove far too fast and shot off the circuit onto the grass. The car dug in, went up at 45 degrees, then the door flew open and almost pulled me out, but fortunately it came down on its wheels and all was well. It could easily have tipped over with me on the ground underneath. Things like that can come to nothing, or you may not survive. The difference between one outcome and the other is tiny."

There were bumps and bruises, for both John and SAL, but nothing major. His enthusiasm remained undiminished. Moreover, he was learning fast, coming to understand not only his own strengths and weaknesses, but also those of the car. In the process, he stopped worrying about what is often cited as the Healey's weakest design point – the location of the steering box way out front, ready to spear the driver's chest in the event of a front-end shunt. "There are lots of stories of people cutting the column and putting in knuckle joints and so on, but in fact the chassis is designed to collapse at the front and only rarely do you get the box moving rearwards. It happened to me years later when I hit the Armco in Italy, but I was unfortunate in that I hit it square on the box. That drove the column back six inches (15cm), which was too close for comfort. What

Scanned from the A-H Club magazine and, unfortunately, poor quality, but priceless nonetheless: champions and stalwarts pose for the camera in 1962, with Frank Walker extreme left and John distracted by the scenery; the caption writer delicately suggested that John Chatham, "was more interested in Christine Wells' award than his own."

TV presenter Guy Thomas awards John the premier trophy at the 1963 Austin-Healey Club dance.

usually happens is that the road wheel hits something, that bends the chassis and that in turn bends the box mounting. The design looks more dangerous than it is."

With Frank Walker whipping them into shape, the 'SW lads' list of competitive exploits grew rapidly and they came to know Healey drivers nationwide. One weekend Frank would march them off to a sprint at Castle Combe, the next a hillclimb at Wiscombe, 8am sharp at Frank's house, or you were consigned to guard duty.

At Wiscombe John often found himself competing against the then Chief Constable of Northamptonshire, John Gott, a popular character who had a quick ex-works car and "took things rather seriously."

"He had a mechanic called Jock Thinn, who worked in the police garage, but seemed to spend all his time working on John Gott's car. I think he was his personal mechanic, 24/7. Things weren't that political back then, so I think they got away with a lot, and good luck to them.

"I quite enjoyed hillclimbing, but there's not enough action for my taste. Last time I ever went to Wiscombe with the Healey 100 I remember clearly that I was fed up with the waiting time between runs and decided to go and have a pie and a pint. And another pint, and another pint. When I came to do my last run, it was fast, faster than I'd ever done before in the car, but when I got to the top, I asked myself, 'How did I do that?' and I couldn't remember. Every time I'd arrived at a corner, the car was there, but my brain was far behind. It wasn't a good feeling, I was not in control. That was a lesson: since then I have never driven in competition with an excess of alcohol in my system." But he'd got away with it, fate had smiled on him again. "I've been lucky," he muses.

"I also did Shelsley Walsh, Prescott, Loton Park, and another hillclimb down in Cornwall, but I preferred sprints. They were often on old airfields, usually local and held on a Sunday. Pursuit sprints were particularly good fun, provided you weren't first, because you had someone to aim at, you could drive like hell to catch them up."

In time, the Austin-Healey Club started to organize its own events such as the Blackbushe Sprint. But then as now, the club was split between those who wanted to use – or abuse – the cars to the full, and those who were more interested in a Sunday morning polishing session followed by a gentle drive to the pub. "Donald Healey was definitely in the first category, he liked to see them used for what they were designed for, he was a motorsport man and he liked to race."

Emboldened by speed events, John too had decided to race. Preparation was an elaborate affair. "I took the bumpers off – it looked rather sporty like that – put chequered tape over the headlights, stuck a number on

the side, blew the tyres up a bit harder and went to play boy racers, feeling just like Stirling Moss." At the time, it was illegal to display racing numbers on the road, "but then in theory you aren't allowed to do a lot of things!" John adds with a knowing chuckle. "In theory you can get done for putting Herbie 53 on the side of a Beetle, but back then, if you had a competition licence, the RAC didn't get too uptight about it."

"My first circuit races were at Castle Combe, but before long I ventured further afield, to Silverstone. On my first race there I'd just fitted disc brakes, and of course I thought I had the best brakes in the world. But they'd supplied me with standard Cortina material, so in a very short race a set of brand-new pads completely disappeared! They took the discs with them too, so that was an expensive lesson."

This was long before Modsports and the later classic scene, and at that time John was entering the 100 in GT Sports Car races. "I did Brands Hatch, Silverstone, Castle Combe, and Oulton Park. Modsports didn't get going until around 1965, and before that I was with essentially production machinery in what was basically quite an old car. It didn't disgrace itself, but it never came first either. Class wins were possible, but there was lot of quick machinery in the 3-litre class and it depended who was on the entry list. For instance, I often came up against a very quick 2.4 Jag-engined Allard, which I never got the better of. I was racing for enjoyment, simple as that."

His partner in crime, both in racing and in the moonlighting that paid for it, was another John. "John Horne was a very good mechanic, and increasingly we would find ourselves going to club meetings all round the country, chasing championships. I was never a dedicated 'pothunter' though, it only really results in another cup to polish. I raced because I damn well enjoyed it, and if I didn't fancy going somewhere, I wouldn't go. Or if something better came up, I'd do that, even if it meant missing an important meeting. I like the water a lot, and if someone invited me sailing and I fancied the idea, I'd go. That was me.

"I had a towing hitch on the back of SAL 75 and I thought of myself as a bit of a jack-the-lad, with my flash speedboat and my flash Healey and my flash bird alongside me. Then Evinrude brought out a 40hp outboard, the biggest you could get at the time, and I put one on my boat. As it had originally been designed for an 18hp, it went pretty well. We tried it out and went water-skiing! Then, coming back at night across the Ilchester Flats after a day's fun down in Poole, I looked in the mirror and every now and again I could see sparks fly. And then everything seemed fine again. This continued all down this straight, mile after mile. Eventually I slowed down and the sparks got worse, so I stopped. I discovered that I'd lost a wheel off what had been a two-wheel trailer. We'd been towing at over 100mph (160kph) and the airflow under the boat was enough to lift the trailer off the deck, except every now and again when we'd hit a bump and the brake drum would ground! We never even tried to look for the wheel, it had disappeared miles back."

There are lots of stories about John Chatham and wheels. "They have great amusement value when they part company with the car, and I've had a few do that over the years. In fact, in the '60s there were a lot of wheels coming off cars. The easiest trap to fall into is to assemble your knock-on hubs on the wrong sides, so that the knock-ons unscrew as you drive. I've never done that, but later on in the Modsports era I did find that J A Pearce alloy wheels work better with the hubs the 'wrong' way round, perhaps because they have a different cone fitting from others: it goes inside the wheel instead of over it."

He also went rallying. They were only local events, but the driving was serious enough. "At that time you could run a nine-rally series round Devon, for instance, on nice roads and have good fun. They were night rallies and they needed to be, because we were flying around at breakneck speeds on what were mostly single-track roads. In the dark, the approaching headlights gave you at least half a chance of avoiding traffic coming the other way. But if there was an unlighted cow just around the bend, tough ..." Eventually, under pressure from villagers and road-safety campaigners, the RAC imposed restrictions, a move which John accepts was inevitable. "They really did have to stop it, because it got a bit harebrained at times."

Just how harebrained is illustrated by a baptism of fire which his new co-driver experienced on a rally in Somerset around 1963. "My normal navigator was James Holman, but he couldn't make it, so his daughter Christine stood in for him. We were haring across the moors near Cheddar and the T-junction with the A38 was coming up, I could see the headlights going along the main road. I knew there was no way I was going to stop in time, so the only option was to put the car completely sideways as we emerged from the side road. We'd have been in big trouble if anyone had been coming, but no one was, and we lived to fight another day. She took it in her stride, she was very cool."

This was just as well, because it was the first time he'd had a female navigator and he wasn't quite tuned in to girl talk. Earlier in the evening, she'd announced that she wanted to "see George," who John assumed was her boyfriend. "I thought she was just making conversation, but after she'd asked me three or four times and crossed and uncrossed her legs a few times, I worked out that George was a pee." The phrase stuck: even today, you're likely to hear John mutter it as he excuses himself from the bar.

A little later he joined another local club, the Bristol Motorcycle & Light Car Club (BM&LCC). It ran hillclimbs at Doddington Park near the M4, where later John would compete in his famous Healey 3000, DD 300, but at this time the BM&LCC's main attraction was its autocross team, a motley crew who competed all round the West Country in wildly differing machinery, including a very quick TR, a hot Mini, a Ford Anglia and an Imp. The Imp driver, Tiny Lewis, sticks in John's mind as particularly able, one of many talented off-road competitors to have emerged from Bristol over the years. He drove works Sunbeam Imps in rallies internationally and was, needless to say, anything but tiny. John describes him as "a great big bugger, about 6ft 6in."

The BM&LCC also introduced him to production car trials. "I did a few local ones, along with all the silly cars that do it – Dellows, things with fiddle brakes, and all sorts – and once I got the flavour of it I did the big ones – Exeter, Lands End, Derbyshire. They were great events, with a lot of miles. The routes meant driving all night, I'm not sure why the mileages were so high, maybe it was just to tire you out, but the Healey did very well. Ground clearance apart, the Healey was good in trials, because it has good traction. People didn't use limited-slip diffs, but a few lads tried welding up the diff solid; it didn't work very well because when you tried to get round a corner you headed straight on into the nearest tree. A locked diff can work if you have the room to chuck the car sideways, scrabble round the corner and then power into the next straight, but on a hill you can't do that.

"My technique, as Autosport reported later, was to treat the hills as if I was on a speed hillclimb. Stones were still falling long after the car had disappeared! But it was wasn't me being a lunatic: it was the only way to get a Healey across the slippery boggy bits. Otherwise, being so low to the ground, the car would dig in and you'd be lost. So we'd just go for it as fast as we could. Anyway," he chortles, "it's much more fun driving quickly."

This kind of driving style was not exactly kind to the car and John concluded that what he really needed was a second Healey, a road-going hack that he could fit with sump shields and the like and use on off-road events. "In any form of sport you inevitably get gradually more specialized. Even then, you couldn't jump into a car which had just won a rally and expect to win a race with it. Unlike now, you might get away with it, but you wouldn't win. One set-up is completely different from the other. I wasn't wealthy enough to have a car exclusively for road

Weston-super-Mare driving tests with DGL 666: note cutaway rear wings.

use, so the answer was to keep SAL for the track, and find a second car for everything else."

So it was that in 1963 DGL 666 entered the frame. It was a late BN1, Bugatti blue when he bought it, and a bit rough. It had also been bent in an accident, so the price was right. It looks very smart today (it still lives in Bristol, painted red and owned by John's wife Vicky's cousin) but at that time suffered the ignominy of having the back of its rear wings chopped off. "I'd landed on them so many times that they were all bent and buckled, so I decided to chop them off and give myself a bit more clearance into the bargain." The fact that he'd cut the bottoms off the back wings did nothing to stem the shower of debris firing out of the back of the Healey, but by then the bystanders had learned to stand well back. It was a case of once peppered, twice shy.

All this fun and games had to be paid for of course, and there was also the small matter of the opposite sex to consider. Work and women had to be fitted in somehow.

Generally speaking, women proved the tougher nut to crack. John's numerous evenings in the garage, and his weekends away, were simply not conducive to a stable relationship. Nevertheless, the long-suffering Jackie, who had become his girlfriend in the Zephyr convertible days, exchanged her bench seat for a bucket when SAL was bought and remained in the picture, John finally marrying her in 1963.

"Her parents were rather protective, so when we announced that we wanted to go on holiday together in SAL 75, before we were married, my parents said yes, but ... We could go away together provided we stayed at a farmhouse that the family often stayed at in Cornwall, because they knew the owners well and they could be briefed to ensure that we behaved.

"So I was put at one end of the corridor and she was put at the other end. And what's more, when we got there the proprietors said, 'we're a bit full, hope you don't mind sharing with another guy.'"

John's tongue darts to the side of his mouth at this point, a sure sign that a mischievous tale is about to unfold. "When everyone had gone to bed, my thoughts turned to the room at the other end of the corridor. But the farmhouse was all creaky, you couldn't move anywhere without being heard. Then I thought, 'if I go along the corridor, pull the flush, and then move very quickly while the flush is still going, they won't be able to hear me. Then I'll creep back into my room in the morning, doing the same thing.'

"It worked like a charm, all week. The only person who noticed anything odd was my roommate, who complained, 'when I wake up, you're never here.'

"'I have to go to the toilet in the night,' I told him solemnly. God knows what he thought of my constitution."

By the time of the marriage, Jackie was used to sharing her man with a Healey. And if she had any hopes that married life would be different, the next few days were about to dash them.

"Naturally, SAL was our wedding car, but on the honeymoon the diff blew. I'd been using SAL in a production car trial – DGL wasn't up and running at this point – and that's very hard on a differential because you'd spin one wheel a lot in the mud and the unit would get hot. This would make the starwheel shaft pick up and shear the clevis pin that holds the shaft. There was then nothing to stop the starwheel shaft gradually working its way out until it made contact with the pinion and locked the diff solid. This was a well-known weakness of the early spiral-bevel Healey diff, and a dangerous one because it could have you going round in circles. In this case I was lucky, the whole diff exploded, so at least I kept control of the car. But I still spent the rest of the holiday not laying with a lady, but laying under the car, replacing the diff with one that I'd found in a local scrapyard."

The couple moved into a flat over Jackie's father's shop in Westbury-on-Trym, John continuing to work at his father's garage. But despite the move, his lifestyle didn't change. "I was far more interested in going motor racing and enjoying my life with cars than I was in playing happy families. I kept

leaving her to her own devices and eventually, of course, she found somebody else. The marriage only lasted about three years and then it was all over."

Bizarrely, it would take another diff failure, almost identical to the one which ushered in his marriage, to sound the death knell of the relationship.

"I was returning from the Derbyshire Trial and I got as far as Birmingham when the diff failed. I decided I'd ring Jackie, tell her I was stranded and ask if she'd come over with a Land Rover and trailer to collect me. It was rather a long way and she made a lame excuse about not wanting to drive a long distance with a trailer in the dark. She said if I could wait till daylight, she'd come up in the morning. So there I was, stuck in this bloody Healey all night with my co-driver John Bristow, who I didn't find nearly as nice to sleep next to as my wife. I later found out that the reason she couldn't drive up to collect me was that she was already in bed with somebody else!"

"I was in no position to complain," he laughs. "I was always a bad boy, I was getting my just deserts. She always thought I was a bit of a wayward character and she was probably right. I couldn't blame her one bit."

By 1966 the marriage was over for practical purposes, though the divorce was not finalized until 1969. Jackie put the kindest gloss she could on it all, saying they'd parted because they hadn't managed to have children, and it was true that John wanted a family, but he feels her explanation was rather more generous than he deserved.

"We parted very amiably, so much so that I continued to live in the flat above her parents' shop, which was just as well because I had no money for anything else, it all got spent on racing."

"A few months after the decree I bumped into her and said, 'I've never had a bill for the divorce.' Laughing her head off, she said, 'don't worry about it, I paid for that, it was worth it just to get fucking rid of you!' We always did get on well."

Sadly, she died at the age of 40 of throat cancer. Then as now, when John talks of her there's no trace of rancour in his voice, only warmth. He was simply too young, and too wild, to make it work.

Back at Egerton Garage, Joe Chatham pretended not to support his son's sporting exploits, but he was secretly rather proud of John's growing list of victories. Funding the sport required more than a mechanic's wage however, so it wasn't long before John started moonlighting.

"We had a row of lockups adjacent to the main garage and I used to fiddle around a lot in those. John Horne and I desperately wanted to go racing, so we set aside winter nights and weekends to work on cars to get more money. I've always been good at making rubbish look halfway reasonable, so I used to buy wrecks and do them up and sell them." Much later John Horne, who still lives locally and still works on Healeys, would work full-time at the garage, but at the time they were just two lads trying to fund a passion.

Officially, Joe still looked askance at his son's competitive efforts, but he continued to support them in his own way. "A lot of the time when he was paying me to work for him, I was actually working on my own cars, and he let me get away with it."

As John's confidence increased and his reputation grew, the two generations of Chathams diverged. "We never really saw eye-to-eye, work-wise, and gradually my side of the garage became a separate entity, and I just did my own thing. It remained one business, but my father did the servicing and mechanical work while I concentrated on buying cars, renovating them and reselling them. I became quite handy on bodywork, and we set up a separate paintshop so that the fumes and dust didn't affect the rest of the premises. And of course, if he got a car in for service that also needed a dent knocking out of the wing, that got farmed out to me."

"On paper, my side of the operation was definitely running at a loss and" – he chuckles – "I know where all the money went!" But at least they could claim all the racing expenses against tax, as it was legitimate publicity for the garage, and on the back of that came routine servicing and mechanical work on Healeys and other cars which Joe was glad to have. And although officially he didn't approve of motorsport, "Dad was a good engineer and we'd often put our heads together over some mechanical problem or other and come up with a solution."

By this time the Healey had been around for a decade and was still very much in production, so there were plenty of owners around with cars to look after. "People started bringing Healeys in for all sorts of work, including a Waxoyl-type treatment – Waxoyl itself wasn't around then – on brand-new cars. Healeys were built to rust and throw away, they certainly weren't built to last. In fact if you look at the later cars, when they were trying to save money, BMC must have asked themselves, 'why paint the bottom properly?' because the undersides had hardly any paint on them at all. Worst of all for rust were the early MkII convertibles, the BJ7s: the metal didn't just rust away, it crumbled. They must have got a bad batch of steel."

It wasn't all Big Healeys of course. Spridgets came and went too, but although John has a healthy respect for the smaller car, it never inspired him in the same way. "I like the torque of the bigger engine. It's not a question of ability: back then the best Sprites and the best Big Healeys always put in similar lap times, and it's still so

Driving tests at Zandvoort in 1962 with the Dutch A-H Club.

today, especially now that so many circuits have been slowed with chicanes, preventing the bigger cars from getting their power down." He adds: "There was one period though, when Big Healeys had a much more limited tyre choice than Sprites, so you'd find the six-cylinder cars disappearing into the distance on the first lap, only to be gobbled up by the Sprites on the last lap as the heavier cars' tyres overheated."

By 1964, just four years into Healey ownership, the pattern of John's life was set. It could be summed up in three words: wine, women and Healeys. Winning mattered too, of course, but though he was hungry for victory, he wasn't hungry for fame. If he had a smart car in the garage, a pretty girl on his arm, some good mates in the pub and enough cash in his pocket to enjoy all three, he was happy enough.

John acknowledges now that this lifestyle held back his competitive career. "It's probably why I was never employed as a works driver. The Healey rally team worked out of Abingdon, but the racing team was run from Warwick by Donald Healey's son Geoff, who was asked many times if he would employ me. He always answered, 'No, the man's uncontrollable. This is a team, we need team players.'

Following the 1962 Zandvoort meeting, John and SAL faced the Dutch A-H Club again the following year, when they were offered a return contest at Crystal Palace.

"Let's face it, he was right. It's all very well for me to say, 'I did it my way,' but with hindsight, it would have been much better if I'd behaved myself at times."

Back then, the priorities seemed clear enough. He'd just come across DD 300 and before long he would meet Sandie. It was a toss-up which he fancied more, but one way or another, good behaviour was the last thing on his mind.

THE GROUNDHOG YEARS

I n 1964, John started looking for a replacement for SAL 75. "The four-cylinder car was never going to be a race winner, and I wanted something that was up the front of the grid, not down the back. That's why I hadn't done much circuit racing up to that point, the car was more competitive in other forms of sport."

He was fond of SAL 75. It was, after all, his first Healey. It had done all that could be asked of it, but the Healey 100/4 was an old design and was now outclassed. Although it had won him club championships and dozens of individual events, "by that time I had so much competition experience with Healeys that club events were like taking candy from kids." John wanted a bigger challenge, and a car to match.

The particular challenge he had in mind was the Modsports series, and the car was to be, naturally, a Healey 3000. In the late 1960s Modsports was fiercely contested and very popular with the public – at most meetings, it was the premier event of the day. Big wide wheels and hairy powerslides made it quite a spectacle. The rules were not restrictive: the original type of engine had to be used, and in the original position in the car, but tuning was unlimited. In the over 3-litre class, the E-Type was the car to beat; a Healey 3000 would fall into the next class down, but as the two classes were often amalgamated to bulk up the entry, the challenge for John was to build a pushrod 3-litre Healey capable of staying with a double-ohc (overhead cam) 3.8-litre Jag.

As ever, finance remained an issue, and one of the attractions of the ad for DD 300 in *Autosport* magazine was that the price was right. There was a good reason for that: the car had been rolled five times at Snetterton by Julian Hasler and was a wreck. "The ad in the magazine said: 'Ex-works Healey for sale, complete, being sold for scrap, all parts available.' I rang up and said, 'Stop, I want to buy the lot, not just bits.'"

He paid £365 for it. Coincidentally, SAL 75 had cost exactly the same. Was this a good omen? As he loaded the basket case that was DD 300 onto his trailer, he could only hope so.

John adds: "£365 was a figure which seems to have chased me through life. Much later, in 1976, I bought an E-Type, which I still have. I drove it home for £365!"

For the same money he could have had the white 100S sitting alongside DD 300 in the garage at St Ives near Snetterton. "It was originally a Sebring car, ex-Moss I think,

DD before it was DD, as works car UJB 143; location unknown.

DD as campaigned by David Dixon.

and it was complete except for a cracked cylinder head." He was tempted, but only momentarily. Four cylinders were no longer enough.

DD 300 was a mess, but it was a pedigree mess. Originally registered UJB 143, it was one of four British Racing Green Sebring cars built by the factory in 1959 and fitted from the outset with hardtops (originally also green) the others being UJB 140 (a test car), 141 and 142. In 1960 the three race cars competed in the Sebring 12 Hours and in the same year UJB 143 made the first of three consecutive appearances at the Le Mans 24 Hours, driven on this occasion by Jack Sears and Peter Riley.

In late 1960 the car was sold to a privateer, David Dixon, who gave it its distinctive number plate, but the car's moment of glory came in South Africa in 1962 when it competed in the Rand 9 Hours in the hands of Bob

DD in the David Dixon era at Silverstone, though not in the hands of David.

Very first meeting after rebuild, a sprint in Gloucester in 1965: absolutely on the limit at a right-angled bend ...

Olthoff, finishing only 3 miles (4.8km) behind Mike Parkes' winning Ferrari GTO after nine hours of racing. David Dixon later sold the car, complete with plate, and after that DD 300 became a regular sight at club events until its career was abruptly put on hold by the mammoth accident at Snetterton.

DD has been raced more or less continuously for the past 50 years in the hands of many different drivers – Stirling Moss and Jim Clark among them – and is unquestionably the most famous competition Healey in the world. Even back in 1964, with a mere five years racing behind it, DD 300 was clearly rather special, so John felt pretty pleased with himself as he trundled into Egerton Garage with the remains on a trailer.

None of that history impressed Joe. "My father looked at it in disgust and thought, 'What the hell are you up to

now, you silly bugger,' probably because he knew it was going to cost him a lot of money. Instead of working for him, I was likely to be working on this pile of scrap."

Joe was, of course, quite right. During winter '64-65 and much of the following season, John laboured long and hard to turn the sad remains of DD 300 back into a car, and to earn the money to pay for it all. To help fund the project, SAL 75 was sold, though DGL 666 he kept for several more years. The endless hours in the garage sealed the fate of his marriage (and of his bank balance), but towards the end of 1965 he did at least have something to show for his sacrifice: his very own ex-works Healey.

He also had, increasingly, the responsibility of running the garage. Joe and Elsie were winding down their commitment to the business and around this time moved out of the house at the garage to a bungalow in

John with DD at Brands Hatch in 1965, just rebuilt and being tailed by the Le Mans Morgan, a long-standing rival.

Winterbourne, to which they would eventually retire. The house was left empty and quickly became a de facto extension of the garage, full of bits of Healeys and other motoring paraphernalia, which had built up over 20 years. One bedroom, however, was kept habitable: after a hard night on the town, it was much handier to crash there than drive out to the flat in Westbury-on-Trym. It also made a convenient love nest.

This set the stage for the entrance in 1966 of the lady who would become John's second wife, Sandie, who was initiated into the delights of life with John in that very room. She must have known even then that living with John would be taxing. Not only was he still married to Jackie, but she also had to share her man with a mistress, the ex-works Healey parked downstairs. Wisely or not, she decided to stay.

Crystal Palace, 1965.

Signalling a problem at Thruxton, 1967.

She did, however, draw the line at living permanently over her predecessor's father's shop. They must, she insisted, find somewhere decent of their own. This was potentially a big problem, because with every spare penny being spent on racing, there was nothing left for boring things like finding somewhere better to live.

Fortunately for John, Sandie's mother came up trumps and bought a flat in Henleaze for the happy couple to move into, so by 1967 the pieces of John's life seemed to be falling beautifully into place. He had a new home, a new woman, an ex-works race car and was increasingly in control of the business that supported them all.

Emboldened by his new status as a thrusting young motorsport entrepreneur, John now started on what was to prove the most successful period of his driving career. Initially the rebuilt DD 300 had looked pretty original, apart

from a colour change to Sebring Blue, and in that form it competed with some success in a variety of events in late 1965 and 1966.

The young Bristolian was starting to make a name for himself nationally. Sometimes at Healey events he would find himself up against the works cars and he frequently got the best of them. This wasn't all about driving ability: although DD was broadly in the same state of tune as the works cars, with triple Weber 45DCOEs and an alloy head, it was essentially a sprint car and could be lightened to a degree that dare not be considered for a factory machine. It would never have withstood 12 hours at Sebring, for instance, but at a club event it was in its element. Nevertheless, the abilities of the driver were clearly a big part of the equation, a fact that was not lost on Team Manager Geoffrey Healey, though the boss consistently

About to lap Richard Cleare's Ace 2.6 at Silverstone, 1967.

held John at arm's length when it came to offering works drives. "Too much of a maverick," he told his colleagues. 'Uncontrollable' was the adjective that kept coming up.

In the winter of '66-67 John decided he needed more grip. "At that time people were just starting to put wide rubber on cars, copying the trend in America" he recalls. He found a set of 8½ inch (21.6cm) wide steel-rim wheels, shod them with Firestone Indy tyres and flared the arches to accommodate them, painting the car bright red at the same time. In this form DD 300 started the 1967 season, but after only a few races it underwent another metamorphosis, acquiring even wider wheels.

"By this time everyone was fitting wide rubber and the RAC had introduced limits on wheel width. For my Modsports Class the limit was 10 inches (25.4cm), but you always stretch rules, so I managed to get some 10½ inch (26.7cm) ones made by J A Pearce," he explains with no hint of embarrassment. "Then it really got fat and low and looked like a groundhog."

In this form the car ran the remaining 1967 events and the whole of the 1968 and 1969 seasons. It was phenomenally successful, as the writer witnessed while marshalling at Castle Combe's Tower Corner in spring 1968. Driving in characteristically committed style, John came second that day, just 1.8 seconds behind Maurice Charles' GT40, the pair of them lapping the rest of the field. In its final Modsports form DD 300, even more than most Big Healeys, was a car you picked up by the scruff of the neck before it had time to argue.

Driven this way, a Healey was indeed a match for

The hairpin at Mallory Park, 1967, DD en route to a win with Gary Nigogosian's very quick Spridget in pursuit.

Castle Combe in 1967, just after the start, with John Lewis in pursuit at Camp Corner.

an E-Type, at least on the right circuit. "With the same amount of rubber, but less weight, a Healey is more nimble than an E-Type," John explains. "I could beat the Jaguars comfortably on tight circuits, but the power circuits were a different matter. So the races I really relished were the ones at Silverstone on the GP circuit, where I had my work cut out."

The motorsport world was becoming very familiar with the burly Bristolian and his hairy red groundhog. After a highly successful 1968 season, *Autosport* put DD 300 on its 21 February 1969 front cover and ran a track test inside by Simon Taylor. The sheer enthusiasm and hard work needed to win week after week is summarized eloquently by this extract from Simon's report, which is reproduced verbatim:

"In 1967 DD 300 won its class in the Fred W Dixon Marque Car Championship, but in 1968, while the other two big red Healeys in club racing – Stuart Hands' and John Gott's – tended to concentrate on individual championships, DD 300 was campaigned anywhere and everywhere, turning up at no fewer than 36 meetings to score its 12 outright and 16 class wins. The cheerful enthusiasm which epitomises the British club-racing driver is present at a high level in John Chatham and an example of this occurred at a Freddie Dixon Championship round at Castle Combe last summer. In practice during the morning clouds of smoke and a five-cylindered exhaust beat heralded the

collapse of yet another piston crown, and John came in, told race control he would be a non-starter, loaded the car up and set off home to Bristol. By 10.45am the Healey was back in the garage and the head came off: damage was confined to the pistons, and John and his two helpers suddenly decided it might be worth trying to make the race after all. At 12.45 the engine was fired up, sounding very healthy, the car was reloaded onto its trailer and the équipe hurried back to Combe – where they just made the grid in time. Oh, and John won his class in the race."

The same article summarized the 1968 achievements: In addition to the 28 wins, there were class lap records at ten circuits all round England. "I was beaten overall by a guy who drove three different types of cars," John adds, "but no one won more in one vehicle."

There was no stopping DD in its final fully developed Modsports form. Here it is at Oulton Park ...

... Thruxton ...

He had long since sized up the driving styles of most of the grid. His main rivals – people like John Miles, Warren Pearce, Jim Jewell, John Lewis, Keith Holland and Aston Martin test driver Bill Nicholson – all knew what they were doing, but the same could not always be said of the rest of the grid. "Some people you could trust implicitly, others you were wary of. Generally speaking, the ones to watch out for were the boys who came along with a lot of money and a nice E-Type that went quick because they'd plenty to spend on it. They didn't have the experience, whereas people like John Lewis and Warren Pearce had thousands of racing miles under their belts."

... and Crystal Palace, leading a Ginetta ...

... Silverstone ...

... and Silverstone again ...

... and finally at Crystal Palace again, where DD holds the 3-litre sports car lap record in perpetuity. Here, it tussles with ex-works car XJB 876, then owned by Stuart Hands.

But even the most experienced cannot remove the element of luck entirely. "For instance, at Oulton Park one day, over Deer's Leap an E-Type had me on the grass and wouldn't let me back on. That could have been disastrous, but fortunately I managed to keep control of the car. When you look back, any incident like that is enough to kill you. I'm just lucky none of them did."

His most serious incident came at Mallory Park in 1968, when a freak storm turned a dry circuit into a river in a matter of moments. DD aquaplaned into the bank and was badly damaged, but John escaped with nothing more than a sore chest. Amazingly, that is the most serious injury he has ever suffered, even although he would go on competing all over the world for another three decades.

John himself took no prisoners on the circuit, but was not considered dangerously aggressive. Off the circuit he proved a wily competitor, adept at bending rules and not above using gamesmanship to tilt events his way. For the most part, he was wise enough to know when to stop, but sometimes his tactics backfired.

His most memorable own goal was at Castle Combe in 1967. "A guy came on the scene, a local driver from around Weston (super-Mare), called Chris Boulter. He'd been winning sprints and hillclimbs in a Volvo-engined Marcos 1800 and decided to have a go at circuit racing. And he was quick: in his first practice for his first race he put himself on the front row between John Lewis in the E-Type, which was a very fast car, and myself.

"John Lewis and I were good mates, we raced wheel-to-wheel most weekends. I said to Lewis that this guy, this young pup, shouldn't be there. 'I've got an idea,' I said. 'You go and tell him what a real bastard of a driver I am, and he must keep well clear of me because I'll run him off the road as soon as look at him.' This was of course untrue. Then a while afterwards, I was to walk up to him and say, 'be careful of that John Lewis, he's a right bastard, he'll have you off the road as soon as look at you.'

"So when we came to the race he had Lewis looking at him from one side of the grid and me looking at him from the other. He was obviously quaking in his boots wondering what the hell us two were going to get up to.

"Now the Marcos, being light, was a quick car round a tight circuit like Castle Combe, but Lewis and I blasted away from him at the start. All three of us got through Quarry with no problem, and Old Paddock, but then we got to Tower. The E-Type and Healey, being heavy cars, had to stand on the brakes hard and early and the pair of us duly anchored up, two abreast, at our normal braking point. This completely took Boulter by surprise: with his much lighter car, he'd got used in practice to braking much later. With us two abreast, he had nowhere to go; he should have

Back at Bristol looking sorry for itself after the accident at Mallory Park.

Castle Combe in 1967, a photo displayed on the A-H Club stand at the 1968 Racing Car Show; Chris Boulter and Marcos hustling Chatham during practice: just hours after this photo was taken the Marcos was scattered all over the circuit.

driven into one of us to absorb the impact, but instead he turned sharp left and went up the bank to avoid us. Chris was unhurt, but the Marcos was spread around the bank in a right mess.

"We carried on racing, unaware of the part we'd inadvertently played in the accident. Trouble was, his father was very upset about our tactics, believing quite wrongly that we'd deliberately braked early to wrong-foot his son, but in no way was that the case. The accident was down to youthful enthusiasm, he was caught out by his own inexperience. If he'd only waited a bit, he'd no doubt have won that race. The brakes on our heavy cars would have gone off a bit and he could have got by."

"It proved a very expensive first race for him, but once he'd built up some experience with different cars, he went on to be a good racer. We had a lot of fun competing against each other."

"We told him later that we'd been winding him up. Many races are won in the paddock and at the bar."

Another bar, this time at Silverstone, played a part in John's most memorable Modsports event. It was a Bank Holiday weekend in 1968, a crucial round of the championship, to be held on the prestigious Grand Prix circuit. To beat the Jaguars at such a fast venue would be a huge achievement, so this, more than any other round of the championship, was a race John badly wanted to win.

"The E-Types were always my stiffest Modsports opposition and on this particular occasion the quickest, driven by a guy called Warren Pearce, was starting from the back of the grid because he'd had an oil leak in practice. This was a lucky break for me, because I knew I couldn't beat him in a straight fight. I was on the front row and scorched off into the lead, determined to make

the most of the opportunity, but I reckoned his car was so quick that he could still come through and catch me – we were using the full Grand Prix circuit, with plenty of straights for the E-Type to get its power down. So I drove as hard as I could, broke the lap record lap after lap, I was really pushing to the limit trying to get away from this guy.

"Unbeknown to me, he'd crawled off the grid at the start and he wasn't in the race! But my pit crew either didn't know this or chose not to tell me. So on I went, trying so hard that towards the end of the race I lost it on Chapel Corner. The back went into the marshals' post quite hard and fast, and my glasses split down the middle and flew off my face. I can't see an awful lot without them – some people say I don't see much *with* them – but I found my way back to the pits where I discovered that I'd had this prestigious race on the Grand Prix circuit easily in the bag, only to blow it all away. I headed for the bar to drown my sorrows.

"It was a Bank Holiday weekend and there was a big party at the back of the grandstand with a bonfire and fireworks, so I went round there and had one or two ales. I got talking to a girl and eventually decided that it would be a rather brilliant idea if I took this lovely charming

The Day of the Broken Glasses: start of the Modsports race at Silverstone, Warren Pearce's E-Type conspicuous by its absence.

"I abandoned the car in the middle of the road with the headlights on." (© Jim Watson)

A Modsports subterfuge at Thruxton: this is not DD! Fellow Healey competitor Nigel Kerr wanted his car to take the lap record on every Modsports circuit, but couldn't crack Thruxton. So John helped Nigel turn his car into a DD lookalike and then drove it to a lap record for him. The organizers never twigged, even though this car has a curved screen and DD's is flat.

lady home with me, so I dragged her to the car. In fact I think she was dragging me, as I wasn't very well by this time and, even if I had been, I still couldn't see what I was doing. Drunk and blind, I had to go down on my knees to get the key in the lock of the Jag which I was using as a tow-car. Then a friend came along and said, 'what do you think you're doing, you shouldn't be driving, and what's Sandie going to say when you get home?' But he could see that she was rather a nice lady, and thought it would be a good idea if he relieved me of her, which he did, and off they went."

In John's mind, there was nothing for it but to try and find his way home. So, damaged Healey on the trailer and damaged ego in the Jag, he gingerly left the circuit. "Every time a car came towards me its headlights made a prism of about 12 headlights, and I just stopped, and thank God, they all seemed to pass me on the right-hand side, which was OK. Occasionally it felt a bit rough and I'd think, 'this road's bumpy,' only to realize I was driving down the grass verge.

"I got as far as Brackley and decided that this was rather foolish and I should park up and go for a walk. I found a phone box and called Sandie. 'I'm alright, I'm alright,' I reassured her. She replied 'I haven't asked you how you are. You're obviously pissed.' And she put the phone down on me.

"After that I sobered up fairly quickly and drove the car back. I got as far as the M4 near Bristol and ran out of petrol. By this time I'd figured out a way to use my glasses:

I taped them together in the middle and stopped them pulling apart by poking the ends inside my crash helmet. So there I was on the M4 about two o'clock in the morning, a zombie in a crash helmet thumbing a lift. Needless to say, no one stopped.

"Then in a flash of inspiration I rummaged around the car and found – hey presto! – a can of petrol. This got me going, but only as far as Filton Avenue, about two miles (3.2km) from the garage, where I ran out of fuel again. There I abandoned the car in the middle of the road with the headlights on, walked to the garage, got a car out, drove home and crashed out.

"Come the morning, I got up, feeling delicate, and quietly tried some breakfast. I'd forgotten all about the car until Sandie said at about 11 o'clock 'you ought to go and get your car, you told me you'd abandoned it.' I rushed up to Filton Avenue where to my amazement I found it exactly as I'd left it, in the middle of a main bus route. It was completely unmolested. No tickets, no problems, nobody said anything, even the headlights were still shining.

"So I got away with the entire episode. I've got away with lots of things in my life. People say to me, 'Your time will come,' but we're still waiting."

Life was good. On the car front, he had a Healey that was winning race after race. On the woman front, the divorce from Jackie was proceeding amicably – which was just as well because Sandie was pregnant. Soon he would be a father at last. What could possibly go wrong?

In the short term, nothing did. Sandie bloomed, John

February 21 1969 2/6

AUTOSPORT
BRITAIN'S MOTOR SPORTING WEEKLY

Amon's Sandown—Swedish Rally—Chatham Healey

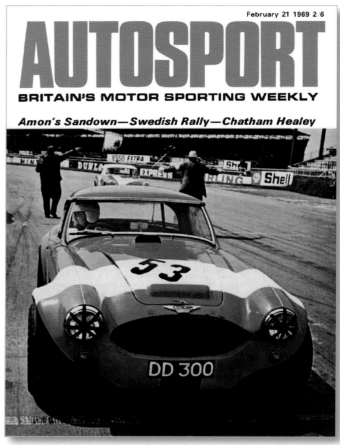

Autosport, 21 February 1969, the first – but certainly not the last – time John Chatham's mount has featured on a front cover. (© LAT Photographic)

SUCCESS YEAR FOR CHATHAM

At the close of the 1967 racing season, Bristol's John Chatham has emerged as one of the country's most successful club racing drivers of the year.

Chatham took up the sport seriously when he purchased a damaged B.M.C. Works ex-Le Mans Austin Healey 3000 two years ago. He rebuilt the car and carries out all his own preparations at his father's garage in Bishopston.

This year, Chatham has recorded 26 wins on circuits all over the country and has broken numerous class records which has gained him the British Automobile Racing Club Freddie Dixon Trophy in the 3-litre class.

Chatham has also put himself well in line for the Austin Healey Club's Clubman of the Year award.

Chatham's biggest feather in his cap this year, however, is the number of lap records which he holds.

Apart from breaking the Marque Sports Car lap record three times this year on the Castle Combe circuit—which he holds, his list includes the class lap record at Silverstone (1min 7.8sec.), Oulton Park (1—56.2), Mallory Park (56.8) and Crystal Palace (64.4).

Now that the racing season is over, Chatham is going to devote his sporting interests during the winter to production car trials and has prepared another car—an Austin Healey 100 x 4—for this purpose.

John Chatham leading the field in a Marque sports car race at Silverstone.

Bristol's Chatham gets the John Gott trophy

The John Gott Trophy, one of the major awards of the Austin Healey Club of Great Britain, has been awarded to Bristol racing driver John Chatham.

The award is presented annually to the member of the club who gains the most positions in 'off the road' events whether they be Austin Healey club events or not.

During the 1967 season, Chatham gained numerous successes with his ex-works Le Mans Austin Healey 3000 and in addition to the many first positions gained in meetings all over the country, he is the current holder of class lap records on five of the country's major circuits.

Following close behind Chatham for the trophy were Alec Poole, a B.M.C. works driver and John Gott, Chief Constable of Northampton and member of the R.A.C. Motor Sport Advisory Committee who also donated the trophy.

Dear Mr. Chatham,

I am a young italian fond of racing cars, and so I have often noted your good races and many victories.

I wish if possible one or two signed photographies of yours with Austin Healey 3000, for my personal collection of motor sport.

I wish also if you know Mr. Stuart Hends' adress.

Thank you very much, and best wishes :

FRANCO CARMIGNANI / Via Dessiè 7 / 00199 ROMA / ITALY

A page from the scrapbook that John kept at the start of his career.

watching with admiration and approval as his petite pretty wife became ever more buxom. Everything was set fair for the baby to arrive on 16 January 1969.

John was not present at the birth – "woman's work" is how he describes that process – and by all accounts it was not an easy labour. But, having assured himself that mother and new daughter Charlotte were finally in good shape, John naturally headed to a Henleaze pub to wet the baby's head, in company with a regular drinking buddy. Come closing time, with the two of them having drunk far too much, the pair rolled back to the flat to sleep it off.

"This is a one-bed flat I'm afraid," John slurred, "but the sofa's very comfortable, I can vouch for that because I often fall asleep on it and get left there all night!"

"Oh no," Drinking Buddy slurred in return, "you've got a nice double bed, I'll have half of that."

"No you won't," John replied, getting less slurred as he got more annoyed. "I told you, you could have the sofa."

"He thought I was joking," John explains after retelling this story, "and he proceeded to get in. So I said it again. 'Now, you did hear me the first time? And the second time? I'm telling you a third time. There is no fourth time. If you don't get out, I'm going to hit you.' He just laughed. So I landed him one straight on the front of his nose. He got very upset, got up and left.

"We didn't fall out entirely, but we weren't so close after that. He realized that if I said something, I meant it."

Fatherhood, John suspected, could turn out to be quite a stressful business.

WATERSHED 4

It took a long time for the responsibilities of fatherhood to take root in John. "I used to call Charlotte my little apple Charlotte," John recalls affectionately, "but I was not a confident father when my first-born came along. However, I had to get used to it as Sandie became pregnant again soon afterwards and just over a year later, on 15 February 1970, I had a son called Joe."

This was not the only big event in 1970. In fact, the first year of the new decade would prove a momentous one for John – domestically, parentally, matrimonially, commercially and competitively.

In preparation for the second birth, the family had found a bigger home, so by the time Joe arrived they were living at Severn Beach, in a house which the couple (by now married) had bought new. In the garage there were two Healeys sat side-by-side: a pink Midget specially painted for Sandie by John and a Sebring Blue 3000 MkIII – pink for a girl and blue for a boy.

The MkIII was a 2+2 version with two minuscule seats in the back, and in 1970 he lent the car to one of his customers, a Bath University student called Al Stacey, for the Rag Queen to be paraded in through the city. It was an act of generosity much appreciated by the students, but one suspects John was partly motivated by the prospect of having a bikini-clad lovely draped all over the back of his car, and having the photos to prove it. On its way to and from the event, the car did of course get thoroughly 'exercised' with none other than yours truly squeezed in the back getting his head blown off and loving every minute of it. Al was a customer because he had a beat-up Healey 100/4 with two claims to fame: the

November 1969, Bath University 'Rag Day' antics in John's Sebring Blue 3000. Fearless stunt man Johann Schultz (aka medical student Stephen Richardson), accompanied by cheerleaders Dawn Fielding (left) and Kay Barnes, arrives at Bath Rugby Ground ready for what turned out to be a carefully counterweighted jump from a scaffolding tower into a bath of water ... (© Al Stacey)

world's most unappealing paint job – an execrable shade of hand-painted bright blue – and a number plate to die for – AH 1004.

Some months later, the same students would find themselves squeezed into an aluminium-bodied MGC GT for an invigorating thrash with the man who had just piloted it in the 1970 Targa Florio, on the excuse that they were writing a piece for the student newspaper. The story of that race, and how John came to own the car, is told later in this chapter, but the Targa Florio is not the C's only place in the Chatham family history. The car also played a crucial role in the birth of John and Sandie's second child, an episode which signalled the beginning of the end of their marriage.

It happened like this ...

One afternoon in February 1970, a phone call came from John Lewis of E-Type fame, an invite too good to miss. Lewis had become a close friend and John and Sandie frequently saw him socially, as he lived relatively nearby, across the Severn Bridge in South Wales. This particular weekend he was planning a black velvet party – a real one with Guinness and champagne, not the cheapskate student version where cider is substituted for the bubbly. Needless to say, John was up for it. Sandie was too, though she was heavily pregnant. The prospect of arriving dressed up to the nines with his once-again gloriously pneumatic wife on his arm pleased John immensely, especially as the run over the bridge would give him an opportunity to stretch his recently acquired MGC for the first time since its completion.

But on the afternoon before the party, his mammary fantasies were ended abruptly by a call from Sandie, who had just rushed from her Midget to a phone. "My waters have broken. I need to get to the hospital."

"Are you sure, how do you know?"

"Because I was sat in a puddle! I need to drive myself to the hospital *now*."

Now a pink MG Midget – or for that matter any colour Midget – is not the easiest of cars for a pregnant woman to drive, let alone an ideal birthing environment. So John rushed off to the hospital to meet her.

He takes up the story. "The staff said, 'you can stay as long as you want, we'd like you to,' but I had other ideas. Sandie's first labour had been lengthy, so I went to her bedside and said, 'I've seen the doctor, there's no point in me hanging around, this could take quite a while and I'll just be in the way. I'll go now, I'll come back and see you later.'

"To be honest, the doctor hadn't said anything of the kind, but I'd just finished building the MGC and I'd set my heart on driving it over to South Wales to give it a shakedown. I convinced myself that there was time to do this, go to the party and still get back to Sandie.

"So I went back home, put on my suit and black tie, and zipped over to South Wales. It was a very good party, so I don't remember much about it, except that when it ended I was in no state to drive. Even if I had been, the weather was very bad.

"Next morning I surfaced around ten o'clock and was gingerly having some breakfast when John Lewis said, 'isn't it about time you got in touch with Sandie?'

"'Bloody hell,' I thought, 'I'd forgotten all about that,' and rushed off to the phone.

"The hospital said, 'who are you?' And I replied, 'if she's produced a child, I think I'm the father.'

"'Oh, you,' came the frosty reply from the nurse. 'Where have you been?'

"'I got a bit ... held up. The er ... weather's been bad.'

"Sandie, the nurse told me, was quite upset that I hadn't turned up. It was obvious that I was not the most popular guy, not with my wife, not with her mother, not with the matron. I really must get back to see her, I thought, but I still didn't feel too good – I decided I needed some hair of the dog and stopped at a pub in the Wye Valley for a few beers. By the time I got to the hospital it was gone three o'clock in the afternoon.

"I don't think the marriage ever really recovered from that," he muses. "It was often remarked upon. Whenever I did anything naughty I was reminded of my worst moments and that was one of them."

Life was changing back at Egerton Road too. The garage still sold petrol, did MoTs and handled plenty of everyday cars, but a regular visitor in the late 1960s would have noticed more and more sports cars on the forecourt as the decade drew to a close. Despite his scepticism about motorsport, Joe didn't oppose this evolution, partly because it would have been pointless – he planned to hand over to his son completely before long – but also because the publicity generated by John's exploits was good for business.

"He knew it was a two-edged sword though," John points out. "Because the better known I got, the more money I spent on racing! For every £1 of extra business the racing generated, I was probably spending £2 extra preparing for the next event!"

By 1970 Joe had worked with his son for fully ten years and, "the pressure of the business, or the pressure of his son, I don't know which, was starting to give him health problems. His doctor advised him to take it steady, 'or you'll be in a box, old chap.' So he retired to his bungalow at Winterbourne and I took over the business completely."

It was good advice, because Joe was only in his 60s at the time, but lived until he was 84. He still helped out at the garage occasionally, but his focus became the shed which he built in his garden to house a Myford Modelmaker's lathe. "Mother fussed about him," John recalls, "saying, 'Joe, put your coat on, Joe, put your scarf on,' but he was always in the shed and it didn't seem to do him much

Joe and Elsie in retirement, outside their bungalow near Winterbourne.

In retirement John's father took up model making. His finest hour was when he made this working steam traction engine.

harm. Maybe the bottle of scotch hidden behind the lathe kept out the cold."

Curiously, although aircraft were his lifelong passion, Joe never made models of them. There were ships, horses and carts, ploughs, a brewer's dray, but no aircraft. Whatever he turned his hand to, the workmanship was exquisite. Every spoke of a wooden cartwheel would be individually machined, with handmade steel banding round the circumference. His models took pride of place at harvest festivals, where the food would be laid out on them.

His finest creation was a working steam traction engine, which John still has. Building it took some nine years, "and if you look at the detail, it's quite fantastic," says John. "He even made the tools to machine some of the components. There were some castings you could buy, like the funnel and the front of the boiler, but otherwise he made the whole thing himself apart from the boiler innards, which he had to buy complete in order to get a safety ticket on it."

Joe still liked to make himself useful to the garage, too, by turning small components, and became a dab hand with ally gear knobs.

John still has the lathe and makes good use of it, but one of his regrets is that he never got his father to teach him to his own standard. "I'd do a job and my finish would be crap compared with his, and he'd say, 'that's because you're using the wrong tool,' or whatever."

Elsie had retired at the same time, so it was all change at Egerton Road Garage. John took on a garage manager, John Smith, to do the work his mother had handled, plus some good hands-on help in the workshop, and then stepped into his father's shoes. "I felt I was ready for it." The name over the forecourt changed too: from now on the business would be known as John Chatham Cars.

The new boss started looking round for a fresh competitive challenge. There was nothing more he could do to DD; it was fully developed and as fast as it was ever going to be. It had brought John a fantastic run of success, but now there was nothing left to achieve. He put the old warrior up for sale.

"In 1970 I briefly sold DD to an American called David Weir. He was a very wealthy young man who used the car as his initiation to motor racing, with me maintaining it for him. However, he campaigned the Healey only for a few months. Before long, he'd got his racing licence sorted, had found his way around the circuits and was looking at bigger and better things. He got talked into buying into a team of Lola T210s and poor old DD was left untouched in the back of my garage. He just lost interest in it."

Even with DD unavailable, there was still plenty of racing to be had, and not only in his MGC. By now John's reputation was such that a steady trickle of one-off guest drives came his way, right through the 1970s. One he particularly enjoyed was at Brands Hatch, where he was let loose with the ex-Le Mans Marcos. It had failed to qualify for the 1968 24h on account of the valve timing being set wrong, but was in good health when John drove it. "The owner, David James, had bought it from Jem Marsh, whom I know quite well, but didn't have the right licence to race at international level, so he asked me to race it for him. It was a Volvo-engined car, an 1800, very different from the Healey, but good to drive."

During that decade, he also raced the Oldham & Crowther XK120 at a Silverstone end of season event, standing in for the usual pilot who was away. "The car was quite nice," he recalls, "but the engine was tired and failed during the race, so I didn't finish."

The issue of Autosport *which featured DD on its front cover also carried this ad for the car.*

A MkII Cobra belonging to Syd Segal was driven in a minor event at Silverstone, though it was something of a disappointment on the track as it was not competitively prepared.

Sometimes he turned down drives flat. Like a tired Healey that had no chance, or a Turner "that was built for a midget, the only way I could drive it was to take the seat out completely."

There were also test days, when proud owners would ask him to let them know what he thought of their baby. The verdicts were not always to their liking: "I drove a Corvette Sting Ray that wouldn't do anything except go in a straight line: wouldn't stop, wouldn't steer, wouldn't handle, an absolute heap, so slow round the circuit it was a joke. A modern Corvette is a good car, and older ones can be sorted, but they take a lot of sorting!"

Much more satisfying was a Porsche 906 owned by Mike Coombe, which John raced at Silverstone. It was his first taste of a properly developed mid-engined racer and

John decided it was a habit he could easily get used to. Indeed, later that year the same car would be their mount at the Vila Real sports car GP in Portugal.

First, however, we must introduce the MGC properly.

No man, not even John Chatham, can live by Healeys alone. By the end of 1967 the Big Healey was out of production and the MGC had been developed as the car to replace it. John had taken a keen interest in the Healey's replacement, not least because the Abingdon factory where it was built was the home both of MG and of the BMC rally team's very successful Healey 3000 rally cars. As the Big Healey's years as a racer had drawn to a close, and with it the Warwick factory's influence, Abingdon became the natural source of competition parts and John had become a regular visitor. Officially, company policy was not to sell works parts to privateers; unofficially the competition department appreciated John's exploits and helped him whenever it could.

The change in focus from Warwick to Abingdon also

Guest driving the Oldham & Crowther XK120 in the early 1970s.

meant that Geoffrey Healey no longer had the last word on who got a works drive. Although John still relished doing his own thing, the lure of official backing and funding was strong and he lost no opportunity to remind the factory of his desire to wear BMC colours. Eventually, in 1969, the phone call that he'd been waiting for came from Peter Browning at Abingdon. Would he like to drive a works MGC GT Sebring in the 1970 Targa Florio? The answer was a no-brainer.

Up to this point John had never owned an MGC, though he had driven one. "It handled completely differently from a Healey: the coupe shell was nice and stiff, but the engine was mounted too far forward, which spoiled the weight distribution. I felt that the car needed to get a lot of weight off the front to make it at all competitive. I was told that to get the footwells wide enough to comply with US legislation, they'd moved the engine 10 inches (25.4cm) further forward than in the Healey 3000, and of course that upset the balance of the car. Unbeknown to me, as I was discussing this with Abingdon, they'd already

cast three aluminium blocks for the C, so they knew the problem was there."

In fact BMC tackled the problem from two angles and built a series of six cars with alloy bodies. These are known as the Sebring cars as two were sent to Sebring for the 1969 12h race. They raced there with iron blocks because the alloy unit was not yet ready, but late in 1969, before the other four could be completed, John received another call from Peter Browning:

"Do you want the good news or the bad news?"

"I'll have the bad news."

"You've lost your works drive in the Targa."

"Who the bloody hell did you give that to?"

"Nobody. The MGC programme is all coming to a complete halt, it's closed down, finished."

"And the good news?"

"I'm allowed to sell you the spare shells and all the parts. There's enough there to build a couple of complete cars."

47

Silverstone late 1970; shakedown prior to Targa Florio.

John drove hotfoot up to Abingdon and after a day's haggling ended up acquiring the four remaining shells – three complete and one in bits – plus two alloy blocks (one of the batch of three had been scrapped in production) and all the spares. The cost of the whole lot was £1500, a bargain even at 1969 prices. Reading between the lines, Abingdon wanted the bits to go to a good home. The two Sebring cars stayed in the United States and were sold there.

Part of the deal was that John would take over the BMC entry in the Targa Florio, something he was more than keen to do, though time was now tight. What had looked like a practical development schedule for the factory looked very onerous for a privateer working largely on his own in his spare time. The pressure was on.

The first casualty was the alloy engine. There is much more to building an alloy engine than simply substituting a different material in the foundry, and the lightweight unit needed development which there was simply no time to do. So John fitted the hottest iron-block unit he could

muster, moved all the weight he could into the boot to minimize the nose-heavy characteristics and worked flat out to create the first UK-registered MGC GT Sebring, which emerged from Egerton Road with a Bristol plate (VHY 5H) early in 1970, ready for its fateful maiden trip across the Severn Bridge.

Logistics followed. "I got Natalie Goodwin of Goodwin Racing Services, an old friend, to handle my entry and I then went to BMC and asked them what hotel they'd planned to use. 'Hotel Zagarella,' they said, so I booked that. Four rooms for four people: me, co-driver Alan Harvey [a Sprite racer from Bristol] and two mechanics – Tim Jewell and my old 'spannerman' John Horne.

"Next we took the C to a Modsports race at Silverstone as a shakedown. It wasn't as quick as my racing Healey but it was solid and strong, a good choice for a tough six-hour event like the Targa. It didn't handle as well as a Healey though.

"Alan had just bought a 3.3-litre Ventora estate and I'd just bought a new four-wheel trailer, so we were well set up.

But as a result we'd spent a lot of money, so we decided we shouldn't spend too much more on our travels – we'd sleep in the car in shifts and drive right through. We stacked all the spares in such a way that the back seat would still fold and allow two to sleep in the back.

"Off we went, early Monday morning and across the Channel. Alan took the first stint, but he got a little lost in Paris so on the Périphérique [ring road] I took over. And when I get going I'm a bit of a terror, I just keep pedalling – no time for food, all I'd let the boys do was grab a Mars bar when I stopped for petrol. But by about 8.30pm we'd reached the Alps, not bad going with a trailer.

"The trip over the St Bernard Pass was quite interesting, as the road was snowy at the top and the trailer was snaking about quite a bit. On the way down I was actually worried whether we'd make it, as the brakes were overheating and the car was getting quite skittish. Alan said, politely, 'don't you think you should slow down a bit?' to which I replied, 'I can't! We've boiled the brake fluid!' But we got into Italy in one piece and stopped to wind down at the first eatery we found, our first proper meal of the day.

"It was all part of my cunning plan: now it was the mechanics' time to drive, which meant I could sleep off the meal in the back of the car, a night-time kip at that.

"Heading for Naples on Tuesday morning, we reckoned we were going well, towing at between 80 and 90mph (130-145kph) in streaming wet conditions, when this Citroën DS went by us at one hell of a lick. We saw him again about half an hour later, beached about 60ft (18m) up on top of a bank, apparently completely undamaged. He must have aquaplaned straight off the road!

"We stopped for lunch in Naples and allowed ourselves to wind down a bit. We'd broken the back of the journey, as we didn't need to reach Sicily until mid-Wednesday. We parked up near an Italian competitor towing a Porsche and the whole group of us went to lunch. Part-way through the meal the proprietor came with a message for the Italian, warning him that we'd be lucky if there was anything left on the trailers by the time we got back, as this wasn't exactly a nice area. But when we returned, everything was as we'd left it. The local thieves must have thought that no one apart from Mafia would have the nerve to leave so much stuff unattended."

Southern Italy in the early 1970s was quite backward as regards infrastructure. South of Naples, the motorway to Sicily was still under construction and the bridge to the island not yet built, so the road was very slow and windy and the team belatedly realized that their schedule was still tight. Nevertheless, there was time for a pizza around 8pm. Still in convoy with the Italian, who spoke very little English, but came in handy in restaurants, the crew found themselves with a table full of enormous pizzas, any one of which would have been enough to feed four. A competition developed to see who could eat the biggest percentage of their pizza, and John, ever game for a challenge, managed about three-quarters of his. No one else got much beyond half.

"When we'd entered the restaurant, there were lots of young men and women inside. But by the time we left the women had all gone, it was almost as if they were under a curfew or something," John recalls. Calabria's social structures seemed as old-fashioned as its road network.

By the time the crew had negotiated the ferry and found their way to Palermo, it was midday on the Wednesday. "Scrutineering was late Wednesday and Thursday, practice Thursday and Friday, so we weren't late, but things certainly weren't as relaxed as we'd hoped. As at Le Mans, the medical was pretty thorough – weight, blood pressure, eye checks, etc – but Alan was so excited that even though he'd had a pretty relaxing journey, sitting there while I did most of the driving, he had to go and lie down for half an hour because his blood pressure was too high. Nothing wrong with his fitness, he was just worked up about the race.

"That was only the first of our problems. Next day we got everything organized in the pits and set off to find out where the road went. The course was 45 miles (72km) – 42 (68km) round the mountains and a three-mile (5km) straight down by the sea – and on a circuit that long there's no chance of remembering all the corners. Fortunately, I'm quite good at driving blind.

"Nevertheless, we took the tow car round to try and get a feel for the place, taking a leaf out of BMC's book who in previous years had got hold of local hire cars and run them flat out round and round the circuit until they'd learned it by heart. The cars were knackered when they gave them back, which is probably why, when we went, it wasn't possible to rent a car at all – the hire companies had wised up!

"Recceing at any kind of pace was not easy as the roads were still open – you could come steaming round a corner and find yourself smack behind a stationary hay cart. At one point we heard what sounded like a clap of thunder and a 512 Ferrari shot past with Herbie Müller driving at race speed, just missing carts, people, dogs ... And practice was just the same! The roads were only closed for the race itself. Mind you, even then they were only closed to vehicles. People still walked around all over the place.

"This was World Championship sports car racing so you had all the big teams there. Porsche had built a series of lightweight 908/03s specially for the Targa, so light that on the unpainted test car you could see the driver through the fibreglass. Each car had a gauge on its pressurized tubular space frame, if the pressure went down they knew they'd cracked the chassis, very possible on this event. The circuit was a bit rough for a racing car, just ordinary roads, and not always good ones at that.

"After our recce we'd settled down to talk race tactics when the organizers came up and announced that we'd entered the wrong class. We'd entered the GT class; they thought we were a prototype. We argued the toss: the MGC is based on a normal road car, no it's not, yes it is, prove it then, how are we supposed to do that, if you can't then you can't race – and on we went. Eventually we found an Italian girl who spoke perfect English and was able to put our case down on paper. This at least persuaded them to let us run, but only in the prototype class. So our humble MGC was now out of the GT category, with its 911s and the like that we might have got somewhere near, and in with the Ferraris and the works Porsches and Alfas!

"Quite why they insisted on this is a mystery to me, it seemed they just had to pick on someone and it was our turn."

(Recent research by Joe Cox, Competition Manager of the Austin-Healey Club, has unearthed a possible reason for the organizers' stance, in that when BMC entered the alloy-bodied Sebring variant in competition, the company always put it in the prototype class.)

"That wasn't the end of the machinations. The local hero was a schoolteacher called Nino Vaccarella, driving a Ferrari, but when the practice times were published, the fastest six laps were all from Porsches. This being Italy, they wanted a nice red car at the front, so something had to be done, and the organizers came up with a rule change that required the biggest-engined cars to be at the front. These, by an amazing coincidence, were the two 5-litre Ferraris!"

"And who was right next to them? One MGC! My engine happened to be about 5cc bigger than the Porsches."

"On race day in Sicily, all the traffic goes one way, towards the best vantage points. Trouble was, that meant we were driving against the flow all the way from our hotel to the paddock. In England that might give you an easy time, but this was Italy! We found ourselves with two lanes of traffic heading for us and nowhere to go. Progress was nearly impossible, the car was getting hot and I was worried about running out of fuel – I only had a sniff in the car as I planned to fill up at the start. Eventually we ran out."

John and Alan tried to get a local policeman to push them with his car, but he wouldn't. So instead they asked him to drive in front while they pushed, switching his blue light on to clear a path. The policeman took one look at the tide of motorized chaos heading in his direction, shrugged and said, "the blue light does nothing." But he put his car in front anyway.

Salvation arrived in the form of another competitor. He had an Alfa in the paddock, but right now he was driving his road-going MG and felt sympathy for a fellow octagon driver down on his luck. Would he nudge them the mile to the circuit?

"But I'll dent your lovely aluminium car!" he fretted.

"Don't worry about that," replied John, "we've come a long way for this, we're not worried about a few dents."

So the MGC rolled into the paddock in something less than style, behind a police car, nudged in with a final shunt to the tail and looking slightly second-hand. It was all very last minute, so much so that when the car was filled with fuel and chose to fire up on only five cylinders, there was no time left to clean the offending plug.

"Our wives were watching all this. They'd flown down for the start of the race and we'd got them paddock passes. All the crowds on the other side of the fence looked across at these sexy ladies in what were by local standards extremely short skirts and got quite excited, shouting and wolf-whistling at them. The girls didn't know whether to be flattered or annoyed – a bit of each probably!"

The start was predictable. An MGC GT firing on six cylinders might have kept a gaggle of 908s behind it for a mile or so, but getting past a C with only five cylinders "took them all of 100 yards!" The car stayed off song right through the mountain section, but when it reached the straight for the first time the plug cleared itself and gave no further trouble.

"In the race," John continues, "I had no real goal to go for, I wasn't going to beat anyone in my class. I pretty soon realized that this was a race to finish, not to win, and decided to settle down and enjoy myself. You could tell when there was sharp bend coming up because of the number of people there, so I'd stick the car in a drift and play to the crowd, with a wave out of the window as I went past completely sideways. Of course the crowd loved this, and after a lap or two there was a big roar every time I came round. This went on lap after lap [the winners had to finish 11 in total, by which time the C had completed eight].

"Then towards the middle of the race I was doing about 130mph (210kph) on the straight when Hans Laine in a works Porsche came past at about 160mph (260kph). Just as he pulled in front I saw the car twitch and a wheel came off. I'd never seen a wheel come off at that speed before – it bounced in a garage forecourt and then so high that it went right over the building – and I slowed,

VHY 5H in the Targa Florio – the tighter the bend, the more spectators crowded round the Armco.

VHY 5H wasn't going to win the Targa Florio, but was certainly capable of entertaining the crowd.

expecting him to do the same. But he just collected the car and drove on, I couldn't believe it! Was I seeing things? Wasn't that a wheel I'd seen just fly through the air?

"I know, I thought, it must be the aerodynamics keeping it stable in a straight line. I'll catch him in the twisty bits. But I didn't – apparently he not only made it back to the pits, he did it fast enough to get the wheel replaced and get away before I arrived. And he'd had nowhere near a full lap to gain that time on me. I was impressed!

"But only a few months later he was dead," John observes ruefully. "Sometimes the quick boys don't last.

"The race progressed steadily for us, with no dramas. We made our driver changes and soon I was back in the car for the last stint, and on the last lap. But I was losing the brakes. If I pumped them, they were there, but they were getting very soggy. Coming down the mountain, it's quite a narrow road and where there are dangerous drops there's Armco.

"Things got worse. Eventually I found myself heading for a tight corner, pumping furiously, but hardly slowing down at all, travelling at what, if I'd had brakes, would have been the right sort of speed. But with no brakes, I was going a bit briskly! The only way round was to put two wheels up on top of the Armco, do a wall of death around the corner and hope to come down in one piece at the other end. I was lucky that the end of the Armco was angled in such a way that I could launch myself up on to it.

"Now the Armco was there because there was a bloody great drop on the other side. Trouble was, there was a lady sat on it watching the race. She saw me coming and – well, she had two ways to go. She could either get run over or jump off down the mountain. She made the right choice, but unfortunately the drop was fairly steep and she broke her leg.

"I didn't know about the injury at the time of course. All I knew was that she had jumped out of the way. There was no damage to the car and I carried on quite happily, though by now the brakes were really suffering."

John eased off a bit, but only a bit. He was still enjoying playing to the crowd and in no mood to go creeping back to the finish line. By approaching corners a bit more gingerly, pumping vigorously and then slinging the car sideways to scrub off speed, he could get round successfully and raise a big cheer to boot.

This technique worked well until he found himself approaching a particularly tight hairpin. He could tell it was a difficult corner as the crowd around the outside was about ten-deep, a sure sign that the locals expected interesting things to happen.

He pumped the brakes. Nothing there at all! No way was he going to get round this one.

"I was getting rather concerned because there was nowhere to go, the whole bend was covered with people. But ahead of these bends they normally had straw bales – if you missed the straw bales, you hit parked cars. There were spectators around the bales too, but not as many as at the Armco. So I pumped and pumped and got a little, but not nearly enough, and aimed the car squarely at the bales. The crowd panicked at the last minute and I remember a bow-wave of people parting to reveal the straw bale, which I managed to hit quite hard, fair and square. One guy sitting on the bale got launched about ten feet into the air – that's how high it looked at the time, though obviously it couldn't have been – his feet pedalling away at nothing.

"On the other side of the bale was parked a brand-new Fiat 500. The bale successfully cushioned the impact, but in the process got shunted into the Fiat, which went rolling down the mountainside. I watched its roof bobbing away as it disappeared out of sight. I assume the car was buggered.

"Everyone was now crowded round the C, including the Carabinieri, and nobody seemed quite sure what do. But I was sure what to do: piss off out of there!

"I'd managed to keep the engine running and I still had oil pressure. The bodywork was fouling the wheels, but not enough to stop the car moving, so I got the car just far enough along the road to be out of sight of the crowd, then stopped to check over the car. The front of a C is quite strong and the damage was largely superficial: radiator and suspension were both OK. The bodywork was bent, but being alloy was easily pulled clear of the wheels. So I straightened it up a bit and carried on to the finish.

"I didn't play to the gallery any more though," he adds with a grin.

Back in the pits, John got word that the police were looking for the man who had "injured the spectator." In fact, John had never touched her, but somehow he doubted that the Carabinieri would appreciate the distinction. In any case, he had certainly injured a Fiat. One way and another, it seemed prudent to make a sharp exit.

At that time, however, sharp exits from Sicily were practically impossible, as the motorway did not exist south of Naples and the local roads were tortuous and slow. There were no ferries either, except across the Strait of Messina. But there were cargo boats willing to put cars on deck ...

Fortunately, they had no need to go to the hotel, as they'd packed everything in the Ventora in the hope of getting away promptly after the race and avoiding the worst of the traffic. So they headed for the port of Palermo and put the whole rig on a big boat for Naples.

Several other competitors had had the same idea – though not, one suspects, such short notice – and after all the pressure of the last few days, the team were glad to be able to relax. "The trip was very pleasant," John recalls, "but I shall never forget as long as I live, the smell as we sailed into Naples harbour, it seemed like the raw sewage from the whole of Italy was going straight into Naples Bay, the most horrendous stink."

The team disembarked with some trepidation, wondering if the Sicilian police had been in touch with their Neapolitan counterparts, but no one paid them any attention. "I suppose it wasn't that high profile. Years later I went back to the island for a retrospective and I didn't get arrested, so I imagine they just forgot all about it."

Although his race result (39th out of 90 entrants) was nothing to write home about, it was respectable considering the calibre of the competition, especially as the first lap was done on five cylinders and the last with no brakes. More importantly, John had enjoyed the Targa immensely. The top drivers, the works cars, the buzz, the atmosphere, he drank it all in. So when later in the year Mike Coombe suggested they take his 906 to the Vila Real GP, a major event in the sports car calendar, he didn't think twice. Two major internationals in one season: 1970 was turning into an unforgettable year.

"On the Portuguese trip the fun and games began right at the start, as we were already running late when we reached the Channel ports and had to take a later ferry than planned. This was before Britain's entry into the European Union (EU), so the paperwork associated with taking goods across borders was much greater than it is now; we needed a carnet to cover the 906 on the trailer and all the spares. But when we got to the French port the guy whose job it was to stamp the papers had just shut up shop for the night. So instead of driving all night to make up time, as we'd planned, we had to kip in our big Chevy tow van and wait for morning. Needless to say, he didn't arrive until 9am, so by the time we hit the road we were really under pressure."

A long hard drive across France followed and even when the Spanish border came in sight the pair were still watching the clock. The last thing they wanted to see were two enormous queues at the border (Spain wasn't in the EU either at this time). Cars were waiting up to an hour to get through, commercial vehicles (including anything carrying a carnet) had to wait anything up to five hours.

John and Mike looked at the two-mile (3.2km) queue of trucks and decided to play their dumb Englishman card – they simply couldn't afford another delay. So the pair sat innocently in the car lane. When, after an hour, they reached the 'jobsworth' at the Customs post and were told to turn round and join the truck queue, they just sat there looking stupid and confused and made as big a deal as possible about doing a '180' with such a big rig. Before long, fearing complete chaos, the officials waved them through out of sheer frustration. Job done, three hours saved, Portugal here we come!

At the circuit, teams were commandeering any piece of spare land, any garage, any workshop they could find. David Weir and his Lola team had it cracked: they'd commandeered the fire station. John explains: "David's mechanics told us he'd simply breezed in and told the

There are no known photos of John driving Mike Coombe's Porsche 906, but this is the same car in the same year, 1970, in the hands of Willie Tuckett – later to be John's team-mate at Le Mans. It was taken at the Jarama 6 Hours when Willie shared the car with its owner and they came seventh overall and second in class. The car behind is Andrew Fletcher's Chevron B8, which he was co-driving with Mike Freaney.

firemen, 'you won't be needing this fire station, you'll all be needed by the side of the track, so you'd better take all the fire engines out of here.' And the firemen just thought for a moment, then said, 'Yeah, you're right,' and proceeded to empty the place!"

Ironically, it was David's team who needed the services of the fire crews, as the leading Lola T210, with Alain de Cadenet at the wheel, had hit the wall hard and burst into flames. Alain got out in one piece, but when the fire crew arrived the scene was, in John's words, "like something out of the Keystone Kops. They turned up, all standing on the outside of this 1930s fire engine, took one look at the inferno and ran away. Before long there was just this lump of molten metal sitting forlornly at the side of the track – no car left at all."

It was a long race – some six hours – and a very hot day. Inside the little bubble cockpit it was warm, to say the least. But aside from being hungry – with so much to do on the Sunday, he hadn't had time to eat since Saturday night – John had an uneventful race until the very last lap. "Our 906 was not exactly a new car and wasn't a contender for outright honours. We were there to enjoy ourselves. We just pedalled on, the car went fine until – practically within sight of the finish line – it broke its throttle cable. All this way, I thought, and nearly six hours driving, to fail at this stage! At the very least, I wanted to be classified as a finisher.

"I fished around in the engine bay, found the end of the cable, then undid the cable at my end. I fed the engine end through into the cockpit and found I had enough length to operate the throttle by hand."

Mike Coombe road-racing his 906 at Vila Real in 1970, the year he co-drove with John. (© Sandra Coombe)

Feeling pleased with his resourcefulness, John crept over the finishing line, keeping well to one side of the track. It was all in vain though: "Because I'd been fiddling around with the car, I'd taken my helmet off and, being so close to the finish, I forgot to put it back on. So I got disqualified!"

By now his stomach was really rumbling, but there was no time to eat, because travel arrangements were pressing. "Mike was taking the car on to Italy for another race, whereas I had business in Bristol and had to get home. So I was on a stand-by ticket to fly back."

"I found a helpful journalist who was just about to leave for Oporto Airport and was willing to give me a lift. We found a hotel near the airport and booked in, too late to get any food. Next morning, we had to get to the airport for an eight o'clock flight, too early for any food. He had a firm ticket, so he got on. I didn't – because of the race, there was a lot of demand for seats.

"The airport was a little 'rinky-dink' place right out in the sticks and the next flight wasn't until four in the afternoon. In the meantime, everywhere shut up shop. So I spent all day walking about waiting for them to open up. With the adrenalin rushing, you tend to forget about food, up to a point, but now it was getting urgent. It was Monday afternoon and I hadn't eaten since Saturday night. I even walked around some of the nearby fields, hoping to find some fruit trees – but no luck."

John finally got away on the 4pm connecting flight to Lisbon, where he had a couple of hours to kill before boarding for the UK. "I stood there in the waiting area at Lisbon Airport, and I blacked out. I didn't feel ill, I didn't feel dizzy, I'd just gone blind! I knew there were some seats behind me, so I carefully backed up, felt for the seat, and

sat down. I realized my blood-sugar level must be way, way down."

"There was a little bar nearby, but all they sold was pasties, bags of crisps and drink, so I had a pasty and a beer. And then another pasty and another beer. And then yet another pasty and beer. The staff must have thought I was crackers."

It was a low-calorie end to a high-calorie season.

Once back in Bristol, John's thoughts turned again to MGCs, but to understand what he had in mind, we need to set the record straight about the fate of the six MGC GT Sebrings.

All six alloy bodies were eventually turned into cars. Of John's four shells, only three were complete trimmed bodies. VHY 5H was his road-legal racer, the Targa Florio car. The second, John assembled to a similar spec, but as a road car. He sold it to Bill Gardner, a local enthusiast from Keynsham; it was subsequently owned by John's old mate Steve Bicknell. The third he built up as a road car for another old mate, Alan Zafer from Abingdon, though as there were not enough parts for a third complete car, a standard MGC GT was cannibalized to finish the job.

The fourth shell was not even assembled when John acquired it and came with no trim parts at all, so once the pressure of the 1970 season was over, John decided to build it up as a lightweight racer, a testbed for the alloy engine. And it was light, as the author can attest, having seen it take shape. Every possible spare bit of metal was drilled away, even the door hinges, the car was like a Swiss cheese. The chassis stopped at the front crossmember, there was no substructure at all at the front, just an alloy nose with the headlamps glued into the wings, while at the back the alloy tailgate was ditched in favour of a fibreglass skin and a perspex window. And crucially, the engine was moved back as far as the shell would allow, four inches (10cm).

John campaigned it in Modsports in 1972-3 and found it fast, but unreliable. "It was quick for one lap. It took the 3-litre lap record at Silverstone, you couldn't get a Healey round in less than 1 min 7 secs, but in that C I could do it in 1 min 5.4 secs." However, for a reason John could never establish, the alloy blocks suffered from poor oil pressure and both engines threw their number 6 con rod. "I got both repaired, but as I didn't have any immediate need for the second one, it got left at the machine shop for several months. When I eventually went to get it, it was hidden away under the stairs behind so much stuff that they said it would take half a day to get it out. 'Come back at the weekend,' they said.

"So I did. 'Where's my engine?' I asked.

"'We put it out for you.'

The lightweight MGC GT Sebring in action, complete with alloy engine – fast, but fragile.

An MG Car Club meeting at Silverstone in May 1992, and perhaps the only time all six MGC GT Sebrings have been together, plus a seventh car (the one nearest the camera) built as a replica. Left to right, the others are Bill Gardner's car, Alan Zafer's, John's lightweight, VHY, and the two Sebring race cars, then owned by Colin Pearcy.

The six original MGC GT Sebrings in action at the same meeting. (© Mary Harvey/MG Motorsport)

"'Where?'

"'Outside.' There was nothing there. It was gone, nicked for scrap."

Somehow, it seemed that fate was trying to send John a message. Lacking the cash or the time to bottom the engine's problems or make the car race-reliable, John sold the unique Sebring Lightweight racer as it stood, complete with its unique alloy engine. At the time of writing it is in

France, in more or less the same condition, though it is not being raced.

As for VHY 5H, that continued to be campaigned in club events for several years, during which time it generated its fair share of stories, including one in the next chapter. Eventually though, it was sold, and its departure marked the end of the C saga at Egerton Road.

"The whole C project was basically a failure," John says wistfully. "It shouldn't have been, the car had potential, as the Sebring Lightweight showed, but BMC never got properly behind it."

LE MANS – ET COMPLICATIONS AMOUREUSE

John had never raced at Le Mans, and no sports car driver can really feel he's made the grade until he's ticked that particular box. Having enjoyed Mike Coombe's Porsche 906, John's thoughts turned to sharing a 911 with him in the 1971 event.

It sounded great. Mike had secured substantial sponsorship, and had organized a team of experienced Porsche mechanics (through the Paul Watson Race Organisation). All John would have to do was buy a suitable car, deliver it to the team for preparation, and then turn up and drive. After so many years as a hardy privateer operating on a shoestring, it would be great to be part of a well resourced team.

John already knew which 911 he wanted, as he'd come across it some months earlier, at the Targa Florio. There, he'd bumped into none other than David Weir, of DD fame, who was sharing with Alain de Cadenet what looked like a nice competitive, lightweight 911, one of only four T/Rs built with right-hand drive. John had talked of buying it there and then, but David wasn't sure he was serious, and soon afterwards sold it to JCB (Joseph Cyril Bamford Excavators) boss Anthony Bamford.

Undeterred, John went to JCB's Uttoxeter premises and, when he had torn his eyes from Anthony's "rather gorgeous" secretary, persuaded Bamford to part with the car. John wrote the cheque, then Mike collected the Porsche and delivered it straight to the team to be fettled for the 24h.

The promised sponsorship, however, never materialized, save that Esso came up trumps with free fuel. A third entrant, Willie Tuckett, was recruited to make

the project more affordable, but nevertheless John ended up with a hefty bill.

So June 1971 found John en route to La Sarthe with Mike, to compete in the world's most famous motor race – at great personal expense, in a car he'd never driven, let alone raced, prepared by people he did not know. The omens were not good.

At the circuit, the 917s expected to front the grid were managing some 240mph (385kph) down Mulsanne; to qualify you had to get within ten per cent of the pole-position time. John's 911 may have been the hot

David Weir's 911, later to be John's Le Mans mount, in action at the 1970 Targa Florio, with drivers Alain de Cadenet/Mike Ogier. The chasing car is the 911S of Sylvain Garant/Bernard Chenevière. (© LAT Photographic)

This painting, given by artist Michael Maule to Willie Tuckett, shows Willie about to spin at the exit of Maison Blanche, and Jo Siffert about to spin in order to avoid him. (© Willie Tuckett)

T/R version (though it was entered as a 911S to avoid homologation complications) but it still had only 2.2-litres to work with. Gaining track time with the car was of the essence. "You get nine hours of practice at Le Mans," explains John, "but with three drivers to learn the car, it wasn't as long as it sounds."

It quickly became obvious that the mechanics were not to be hurried. Scrub in the tyres, bed in the brakes, do this, do that. Fine, if your drivers are intimately familiar with their machinery and know the circuit. But these pilots urgently needed track time. The mechanics plodded on. The hours ticked by.

"I was getting more and more disgruntled. I'd never driven the car, our job was to get out there and get some times in."

Eventually John's patience was exhausted. "'Hold on,' I interjected, 'I've not driven this car. I've come here to qualify for a race, not piss around bedding-in brakes and tyres. In 24 hours we've got lots of time to do that.'"

Finally, the 911 left the pits. But out on track the Rodriguez 917 was going faster and faster, raising the qualification bar higher and higher. Mike drove, Willie drove, but the faster they went, the faster Rodriguez went. Qualification remained elusive.

Then Willie tried too hard at Maison Blanche and spun in the kink at about 130mph (210kph) right in the path of Jo Siffert's 917 which was doing some 200mph (320kph) at the time. With such a huge speed differential and no room for manoeuvre at all, only Siffert's great skill prevented a horrendous pile-up, the 917 driver managing to spin onto the grass and thus avoid a collision. Tempers ran high in the pits afterwards and things were in danger of getting physical until the marshals intervened. Willie doesn't blame Siffert for being angry. "I drove in many races with Jo Siffert and always found him to be a real gentleman, but on this occasion he probably did have good reason for his blood pressure to burst!"

At long last it was John's turn to take the wheel. "When

Skid marks on the circuit tell their own story of the Tuckett/Siffert incident. (© Willie Tuckett)

the car was handed over to me, there were only two hours of practice left. And it was going dark. The first flying lap I did, I was three seconds quicker than either of the other two drivers. On the second lap I improved. But on the third lap I went a bit slower because the car was losing 200rpm on Mulsanne – we found out later that there was a valve train problem. As I came past the pits they were all jumping up and down and I thought, 'what the hell is wrong?' so next time round I came in. I reckoned I'd had the best out of the car anyway.

"They said, 'what did you come in for?'

"'What were you jumping up and down for?'

"'Because you were a tenth of a second off qualifying! You were going so well.'

"'So you're excited? Well I'm pissed off. There's the car, you do it. I cannot go quicker in that car, that's it. I know how fast it goes round, it cannot be done.'

"I'd just had enough. The whole event was one big disappointment."

John Chatham's 911T/R parked in the paddock at Le Mans next to Mike Coombes' transporter. (© Willie Tuckett)

Stunned by John's anger and knowing he was quicker than either of them, neither Mike nor Willie even attempted another lap. That was it, finished. Le Mans 1971, J Chatham, M Coombe, W Tuckett, DNQ.

Someone said dejectedly, "I suppose we'll just have to watch the race," to which John replied, "I know what I'm doing. I'm going to put the car on the trailer and piss off. I came here to drive, not watch a fucking race. I'd get very angry, watching a race I should be in."

Mike would have liked to stay, but realized that the root of the problem lay in the organization, which he'd been in charge of, "so he felt a bit bad about it." Seeing that John was not for turning, he didn't argue. The pair of them loaded up the Porsche and set off for Bristol, their Le Mans dream over, but their friendship intact.

"They – the team that is – wanted to take the car back to their workshop 'to check it over' and – I suspect – because they were worried about getting paid and possession is nine-tenths of the law. They did get some money, but they were never paid in full, because they pissed me right off."

Despite the debacle in France, John liked the 911 and hung on to it for a while – after fixing the oil-feed to the rockers which had dulled its performance at Le Mans. "It was blue with an orange stripe. I happened to see an all-orange one and casually remarked that it looked good. It was just a throw-away remark, nothing more.

"Mine needed repainting and the staff agreed to do the job while I was away on holiday. When I got back they'd painted it all orange as a surprise! And I hated the car after that!"

Then the car developed a misfire and, as John's enthusiasm for the 911 was waning, his attempts to trace the fault were half-hearted and unsuccessful. The car gathered dust at the back of the workshop and eventually a friend asked to buy it.

"Give me two grand," said John. The deal was done.

"This guy was a bit of a wheeler-dealer and within two or three weeks he'd sold the car for about four grand. Within a month it was for sale for nine grand, within two months of that it sold for 35 grand, and within a year it was sold for £165,000! Mostly because it was an ex Le Mans car! That never qualified for the big race!"

John is philosophical about it. "In the end, I was happy just to get rid of it."

The abortive foray to Le Mans did have one positive outcome, for at the circuit John had met up with David Weir again. "He turned up with a 512M Ferrari, bought from NART (North American Racing Team) and entered by David Piper. But he announced that Le Mans would be his last race: he'd spent his budget, he was finishing with racing, he was going back to America after the race and never coming back to Europe again because it sucked all his money up."

And, after a creditable fourth-place finish at Le Mans, he did exactly that. John didn't see or hear from him until later that year when he turned up at Egerton Road and asked to have DD back. "He seemed to be wandering around Europe," John recalls, "trying to pick the pieces of the trail of debris he'd left. In addition to DD, there was a Daytona Ferrari to be accounted for in Paris, and I think there was 275 GTB somewhere too. He had a lot of money and if he crashed a car or blew the engine, he'd just bought another one."

David may have wanted his car back, but John was in no mood to let DD go a second time. "It's my car now," he replied firmly. "You left it here for years, with a debt owing to me, so I took it back, rebuilt it and now I'm racing it."

"Well," David replied, "as long it's being put to good use, you're welcome."

"And that's the last time we ever spoke."

What David Weir hadn't known until that point was that John had been putting it to good use for quite a while. Towards the end of 1970 John had taken a long look at the old racer gathering dust in the back of his garage and decided that its competitive career as a Modsports car was over. Putting aside the minor detail of who actually owned it, he proceeded to rebuild the car to its original 1960 spec, complete with green paint and standard wheels, in preparation for a new career as a classic racer. "I wanted it to look like it did when the works campaigned it in 1960."

To help him, he turned to Nick Pride, a mechanic whom he'd taken on around 1968. Nick had left to work in Holland in 1969 and had come back to the UK with a distinctly laid-back approach to life. Now John asked him to return as a freelance and rebuild DD. As Nick had just split up with his wife and had nowhere to live, John found he got more of Nick's time than he bargained for, Nick arriving for work at Egerton Road complete with sleeping bag. Over the next few months he literally slept on the job. Later, in 1976, he insisted on working all summer long in bare feet. Other employers would never have given him so much licence, but John has huge respect for his fastidiousness and his willingness to think around a problem as well as through it. Nick still works for John today.

For John in 1971, times were changing. Now, DD was not the only mistress tempting John away from his family, because he was also involved with Porsches and MGCs. Henceforth, DD's racing career would be less intense than the glory years of '68-69, not just because John was

DD in a club meeting at Thruxton around 1972, after being returned back to works spec.

campaigning more than one car, but because its owner's priorities had changed.

"You go through a period in your life when you're racing every weekend because it's in your blood, and you just want to be there. On a Bank Holiday weekend, I could drive to Silverstone on the Friday night, do a race on the Saturday, rush off to Brands Hatch or Lyddon Hill on the Sunday, and then come back to Silverstone to do another race on the Monday. It was intensive racing. I enjoyed it at the time, but you grow out of it. Obviously, if you tried to compete at that kind of pace today, with today's traffic, it would be suicidal, but even back then it could be tough going. You start to fancy the idea of a good weekend away, in one place, somewhere like Montlhéry, with slightly longer races and more fun."

As classic racing developed in the 1970s, John made the most of the opportunities. The Austin-Healey Club wasn't yet organizing its own sporting events, but the Thoroughbred Series sponsored by Oldham & Crowther was popular and John had a lot of success in it.

In Thoroughbred spec, DD ran initially on steel wheels, but these did not stand up well to the high cornering loads of racing and in 1971 one suffered a fatigue failure which prompted John to write to *Motor Sport* about the need for a source of standard-width wheels in good-quality materials. In the meantime, he replaced them with Minilites mid-season, arguing that Minilites must be original because the factory had rallied with them. Despite some harrumphing from the historic fraternity, he kept them on for the 1972 season and went on to win the championship on them; only later did he substitute wires. As a result of the championship victory, DD carried

DD in action around 1977. (© Fred Scatley)

number 1 throughout 1973. At other times it could be seen carrying 69, the number John always tended to opt for, given the choice.

International events were developing, too. DD made trips to Zandvoort, to the Spa Six Hours, and to the Coupe de l'Age d'Or at Montlhéry, the latter becoming a particular favourite. John won the event outright in the 1970s and much later, in 1984, had a fantastic race when DD got very physical with a trio of French E-Types, coming second overall behind Ganzin's example, and first in class. In John's eyes the Jags were illegal because they had fibreglass bonnets, but their drivers, in turn, countered with an allegation that DD had the wrong brakes ...

For the Bristol Healey contingent, Montlhéry became known as a good crack and a number of club members would go along to spectate and to party. Among them was John Simcock, who, like many people in John Chatham's life, started off as a customer, but evolved into a friend. By the mid-1970s, John had been looking after Simcock's 3000 MkIII for some three years and the pair knew each other well.

Simcock recalls: "When John won in the '70s he was towed from bar to bar in DD, with his champagne glass getting refilled at every stop. Then on the way home we fancied a top-up and found a nice little cafe in a small town. Trouble was, the whole of the square was double parked. So we just triple parked and headed for the bar.

"We were probably pissed when we went in, we were certainly pissed when we came out, and as we walked up to the Range Rover and trailer there was a Gendarme standing next to it. John looked at him, he looked at John. We sensed a ticket, at the very least. He said, 'Austin-Healey,

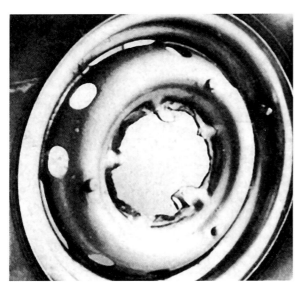

The failed front wheel of John Chatham's racing Healey 3000, DD 300, mentioned on page 526. Standard wheels are mandatory in Thoroughbred racing. Chatham has written to us: *"In the interest of safety we would like you to help press the case for wheels suitable for current speeds and tyre compounds, that is wheels of the same dimensions in alternative materials"*.

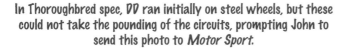

In Thoroughbred spec, DD ran initially on steel wheels, but these could not take the pounding of the circuits, prompting John to send this photo to *Motor Sport*.

Distracted at Thruxton, about 1972.

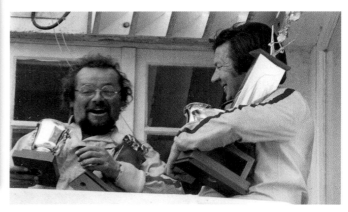

On the podium at the Le Mans Bugatti Circuit after winning the Coupe de l'Age d'Or, with John Harper.

very good.' Then he added the immortal words, 'I have an Austin-Healey,' and helped us manoeuvre out of the square! What were the chances of that square being policed by a Healey owner? It's the luck of Chatham!"

Simcock might envy John's seemingly endless supply of good luck, but later that day he too was glad of it. Flat out in an alcoholic slumber on the ferry, Simcock couldn't be roused to go and present his passport to the purser. John took it for him, but the purser was having none of it. "I need Mr Simcock to present it in person," he explained firmly. John summoned up the most engaging grin he could muster, looked him straight in the eye and said, "Come on! You know what the ugly bugger looks like." The purser wilted. He stamped the passport.

Simcock recalls another brush with authority on their travels back from the Continent. "We were returning through UK Customs and got pulled over, not unusual as they tended to be interested in Range Rovers stuffed to the gunwales with racing paraphernalia and Healey spares and towing racers on trailers. But you could sense the Customs man's mind working: 'If I go to town on this lot, it could take hours, and it's late on a Sunday night ...' So he tried what I'm sure was a test question about the trailer, which was running on Minilites. 'A trailer? On Minilites? I bet those were fitted in France ...'

"He got a detailed answer about how they were very early Minilites, and how you could tell their vintage by this, that and the other – after which he just waved us through. He must have thought, 'these people can't be smugglers, they're just idiots. They put valuable alloy wheels on a bloody trailer!'"

Despite this emphasis on bigger venues, it wasn't all sunshine and glamour. If he fancied it, and had nothing else to do, it was not unknown for John to ask for an entry to a local club sprint, just as he'd done 15 years before. And he regularly attended the Austin-Healey Club's

'Le Grand Pilote,' as he was known in French historic racing circles, shows off his silverware after victory in the Coupe de l'Age d'Or; the year is not certain, but is probably 1971.
(© John Simcock)

Elsie, John and Sandie with toddler Charlotte and baby Joe, 1970.
(© Sandie Savory)

annual social weekend on the Isle of Wight, although as it was in October his entourage was often on the small side. Simcock, for one, was not a fan: "we always ended up in some horrendous B&B and the weather was always damp and foul."

Nevertheless, there were signs – only signs, mind you – that the 'bad boy' was growing up.

With two children to support, the Chathams had already decided they needed a bigger house, so although they'd only lived there a couple of years, the property at Severn Beach was sold in 1971 in favour of a house in Egerton Road, right opposite the garage. When his father had moved to Egerton Road with two children in 1952, he'd been down to his last few shillings. Now his son had done the same thing, but in utterly different circumstances – as good an indication as any of the way the country's prosperity had changed in the interim.

"That was a great house, a big Victorian place with lots of space, which is what caught my eye. I could park 12 cars in the driveway and I had undercover space at the end of the garden for another ten."

With the family safely ensconced right opposite, John no longer had any need of a 'crash pad' at the old house. In fact, he concluded that he no longer needed the old house at all, and before long he decided to pull it down to make room for an extension to the garage.

"A very good friend of mine, Tony Fowles, owned a Healey and was in the scaffolding business," he recounts. "I applied for a new build on the corner of the garage and it was granted, but I knew nothing about demolition. I just rang Tony and asked him to put scaffolding round the house, which was right on the corner of Egerton Road and the main A38.

"So he got the scaffolding up and one Sunday morning I started to pull the house down. I'm there with a sledgehammer, standing on the ceiling so I can knock the roof off, when the ceiling collapses and leaves me holding a 14lb (6.4kg) sledge in one hand and hanging onto a purlin with the other, with nothing underneath me. Fortunately I had the presence of mind to let go of the sledge, grab hold with two hands and scream for help from the friend who was helping me. He came along with a ladder and helped me down.

"By the time this little escapade was over it was Sunday lunchtime, so we decided it was time to adjourn to the pub. Later we emerged and knocked some more down, but it all seemed to be taking a long time, so eventually, after we'd taken quite a section off, I decided the best thing to do was put a rope through the upstairs window, then round through the downstairs window and attach it to a chain on the back of a Range Rover. Then I could drive away and pull the whole side wall down – much easier!

"We had differing views about what was likely to happen. He thought the top would come off, I thought it might be more interesting than that. In fact, as I gunned the Range Rover, the masonry came away from the bottom and as I looked in the mirror I saw a whole wall, the height of the house, chasing me! All I could do was give it as much wellie as I could and hope the big bits missed me.

"They did, more or less, though there were bits of debris heaped all over the back of the car. The wall landed right across Egerton Road and blocked it completely. This was a big old stone-built property – the headstone over the door read 1861 – so there was a lot of wall. As the dust cleared and I surveyed the scene, I thought, 'you were lucky to get away with this.'

"By the time we'd made the place look vaguely tidy and cleared the road, we'd had enough for one day. The roof was pretty well knocked off by this time, but the front wall was still there, on the main road, with the scaffolding tied to it.

"I had no intention of pushing my luck a second time and blocking the main A38, so a few days later I tackled the front wall, bit by bit, working my way down the scaffolding. By the end of the day I felt quite pleased with myself – house all gone and no one inconvenienced.

"Then I had a phone call early one Monday morning from Tony. He'd had a call from the police about some unsafe scaffolding standing on Gloucester Road and in danger of falling down. I couldn't work out what the problem was, but he came along to inspect anyway.

"Tony took one look at it and said, 'you silly bugger, as you pull the building down you're supposed to take the scaffolding down as well!'"

John had simply left the scaffolding standing there and, with no building left to support it, the tube work was swaying in the breeze every time a Bristol Lodekka (bus) rumbled past on its way up to Filton. "So Tony set to it with his workers and carefully dismantled it all.

"Shortly afterwards I got a call from the Council. 'We understand you've pulled a house down Mr Chatham.

"The tube work was swaying in the breeze every time a Bristol Lodekka rumbled past on its way up to Filton." (© Jim Watson)

Where's your demolition certificate?' I said, 'What demolition certificate?' I didn't know anything about them. So I got a rap on the knuckles about that." Considering all the disasters that could have occurred, John had got off extremely lightly – again.

John had earmarked the site of the house for a car showroom, but faced with various building and planning complications, decided he didn't need a retail outlet after all and rented the site to a second-hand car dealer called Mike Savory.

Before long, the car lot wasn't the only part of John's real estate that Mike was occupying. By now, John's second marriage was well and truly on the rocks, with John living downstairs and Sandie living upstairs, and by 1972 things were very frosty indeed. John was relieved when Sandie got friendly with Mike, even though he didn't like him much and was often tempted to add two letters to the front of his surname, and was positively delighted when in 1973 Mike moved in upstairs. With his de facto separation turned into a reality, John was now free to resume – or to be precise continue – doing his own thing.

Downstairs, friends and lovers came and went and it was not until three years later, with Sandie and Mike still living in the top half of the house, that one woman started spending much more time downstairs than any of the others. The lady who was destined to be John's third wife, Vicky, had entered the frame.

However, her story belongs to the next chapter, because in the interim there was the small matter of a divorce to contend with, and the future of Charlotte and Joe to be considered. Eventually, Sandie and Mike moved to Downend with the children and John had the house to himself again.

"I suppose Sandie and I were never that well suited," John observes with the benefit of hindsight. "She always seemed to see the dark side of life and not the bright side, just the opposite of me. I'll never forget one incident in the Alps on the Italy-Switzerland border. Fantastic view, fantastic day, snow on the mountains, open Healey.

"'It's cold,' she complained.

"So we stopped to put the hood up. It was quiet, it was beautiful – God's country. The view was awe-inspiring and everything was so peaceful. I said, 'aren't you going to get out of the car and have a look? It's stunning!'

"'Oh, hurry up,' she snapped, 'we've got a ferry to catch.' She couldn't see the beauty around us.

"In many ways," he continues, "the relationship was a case of 'out of the frying pan, into the fire.' Jackie's way of explaining our break-up, and dealing with the fact that she had trouble conceiving, was to bandy it about that I couldn't have children, and that only made me all the keener to find someone to have children with – hardly a sound basis for a marriage, though it all seemed to make sense at the time."

Even without this shaky foundation, John acknowledges that anyone he married at that time would have had, at the very least, a challenging time. "In those days the ladies of my life didn't seem to last too long, probably because I spent so much time in love with my mistresses, my cars."

And it wasn't just *his* mistresses he had to look after. Customers had their own passions and enthusiasms that John was expected to share, although he found that easier with some cars than others. "One of my customers had an Elan +2S in the early '70s and I looked after it for him, a very pretty car in metallic maroon with a silver roof. But it was like a homing pigeon: it never seemed to leave my garage! There was always something wrong with it. I was never a great fan of Mr Chapman; although some of his ideas were very good and some of his cars were quick, they always seemed too frail."

More to his taste was an AC Ace 2.6, in the garage for a routine tracking adjustment and belonging to the man who would much later write this biography. To be precise, it was the number plate which caught John's eye: 661 CGT. Just the thing for a hairy MG. Then as now, neither car nor plate were for sale, but that didn't stop their owner stopping by occasionally. John Chatham Cars was the kind of place where there was always something interesting going on, and where projects that no one else would consider, would at least be given a fair hearing.

So when an acquaintance of the author's acquired what appeared to be a beautiful maroon Ford Consul Convertible, but which was horrendously rotten underneath on account of having lived near the sea, it was to Egerton Road that we naturally gravitated.

The underside was in a shocking state, so bad that if the you tried to enter on the driver's side, your weight would buckle the chassis and you couldn't close the door. John watched us slide across from the passenger's side, poked around underneath, played with his beard for a few moments and then pronounced: "well, anything's *possible*." We soon concluded that repair was hopelessly uneconomic, and it never happened, but he'd given the job some thought, and taken us seriously, in a way that few other garages would.

The business may have changed its name to John Chatham Cars, but its location hadn't altered. Situated on one of the main arteries into the city and in the centre of a large residential area, it had thousands of houses in every direction, most of them with a car parked outside. Its proprietor had only to do a decent job at a fair price

to be guaranteed a living. So there was always a steady stream of routine maintenance to do, plus MoTs and petrol sales. And it was the busy MoT bay which gave John the most grief, so much so that at one point he considered abandoning non-specialist work altogether. "I just couldn't handle people bringing in a pile of junk and then coming up to me and saying, 'why have you failed my car?'

"What you actually wanted to say was, 'because it's no bloody good, that's why,' but of course you couldn't, you had to search around for a polite way of saying the same thing. You got so many dumb questions: if it had a rusty brake pipe and had to have a new one, they'd say, 'why is it rusty?' and I'd have to take a deep breath and say patiently 'because it's made of steel, and that rusts.'"

Little by little, he eased the business into the specialist market, but John resisted the temptation to rely on it, knowing precisely which side his bread was buttered on. Everyday service and MoT work paid the bills; the classic car business, by contrast, tended to consist of a few large jobs, the loss of any one of which could make a big dent in the year-end figures.

At this point we must introduce a man who has become one of John's closest friends and, as a result, a Healey racer of some repute in his own right. Steve Bicknell's first taste of the Austin-Healey marque was in the late '60s, when he owned a Frogeye Sprite with an Ashley front, but the acquisition of a Big Healey, plus the purchase of a car from Mike Savory, brought him into John's orbit and the two gelled immediately.

"John was a playboy when I met him," Steve remembers. "All he did was work, drink and race. But then we all worked hard – six days a week, most of us – and played hard. In the 1970s, all the bouncers at all the clubs knew us, and we never seemed to have to pay to get in, but then some of them would turn up at the garage wanting a favour ... We knew no harm would come to our cars in the evenings, it was a great atmosphere.

"Without John I probably wouldn't have gone motor racing the same way. After I completely messed up my knee playing competition squash, I'd asked myself, 'What do I do now?' And as I already had a Healey and knew John, the answer was obvious. John was a big influence on a lot of people having Big Healeys in Bristol. And as Bristol is a pretty nice city to live in, people tend to stick around."

When he met John, Steve was already in business, buying and selling classics in a small way with Bruce Collins – coincidentally an ex of Vicky. When Mike Savory moved out of the car lot around 1979, Steve took the plunge and went into car sales with John full-time, trading as J&S Cars. The idea was that Steve would buy and sell and run the car lot, while any work needed would be contracted to John Chatham Cars in the garage next door.

"But it didn't really work," Steve explains. "I'd say, 'I need this car tomorrow,' and John would say, 'Sorry I've got this and that to do first.' So the pair packed the partnership in after only a couple of years, before the business threatened their friendship, at which point Steve renamed the site Bicknell Cars and simply paid John a rent. "We got along a lot better that way."

In March 1975 Steve and John decided to go on holiday together to celebrate John's 35th birthday. They were joined by two other friends, Howard Lambert – a semi-precious metal dealer from London – and Colin Stodgell. "Quite an odd crew," Steve recalls, "but we all got on very well." The original idea was to fly Swissair to the Rio carnival, as Steve's parents had access to a flat there, but the Brazilian authorities insisted on tourists buying flight and accommodation packages through Varig, including full-board hotel accommodation for every night of their stay. This made the whole trip unaffordable.

So the foursome changed tack and went to Mombasa in Kenya for three weeks, to a good hotel which, because it is still very much in business, must remain anonymous.

On arrival, the first priority was to find the bar, the second to see if there were any unattached females in it. There was only one, a local girl, "with her tights joined at her knees." She was certainly never going to win any prizes for dress sense, but heck, it was Hobson's choice. The others bet John he couldn't – or rather wouldn't, for an approach was clearly unlikely to be rebuffed – successfully chat her up. A tempting kitty was soon on the table.

Ever game for a challenge, John sauntered over to the bar. "She wasn't very pretty at all," he recalls, "but as the evening went on, she got much prettier. We couldn't communicate very well, because she only spoke Swahili," but some communications don't need words, and in what seemed like no time at all the pair had disappeared to John's chalet on the beach, leaving the other three feeling somewhat stunned by the sheer pace of events and wishing they hadn't been so rash with their cash.

Hurrying behind the two figures heading to the chalet were two of the hotel staff, who had been watching with interest and wanted their commission on the deal. If John had had any doubts about the girl's reasons for being in the bar, they were certainly dispelled now.

"It turned out she lived in a mud hut," John related later. "I think her main motive was to enjoy a good bath – she certainly needed it – and a night in a nice comfortable room. You couldn't blame her really." The kitty went to a good home.

The group had decided that each week they'd go

somewhere away from Mombasa, where they were based. "In the first week we flew to Zanzibar, where it seemed the four of us represented 80 per cent of the tourists on the island!

"The following week we decided to go to the Ngora Gora crater in Tanzania. We didn't want to join a tour party, so we rented a Peugeot 404. It was white with a column change." The 404 had proved a formidable competitor on the Safari Rally, so it was a good choice. But the hire rate went up if you went outside Kenya, and also there was a fairly stiff high-mileage charge, so somewhere near Lake Manyara John in his wisdom decided to disconnect the speedo.

The hire company, being wise to this ruse, had put a locking device on the back of the speedo. But as John observes, "there are two ends to a speedo cable. So I found a big lump and drove the car up on to it so that there was loads of ground clearance, then crawled underneath and unbolted the bottom end.

"You had to check in as you entered the national park surrounding the Ngora Gora crater, because the authorities wanted to make sure everyone came safely out. We stayed at a hotel that hangs right on the edge of

Sword fighting with Steve Bicknell on the beach in Mombasa in 1975, the only time since 1965 that John has been without a beard.

the crater, which is a defunct volcano, extremely deep and ten miles (16km) wide."

It was a stunning place. "In the morning you could look down on the animals which were so far down they looked really tiny."

Steve Bicknell takes up the story. "We had a very good time there and fancied going to Mount Kilimanjaro on the way home. None of us fancied climbing up, so we decided to drive the Peugeot up as far as we could. We carried on quite a bit after what you would even remotely call a road had disappeared. The surface was just shale. The 404 was only two-wheel drive, but I doubt if a 4x4 would have done much better. Needless to say the Peugeot found this quite hard work.

"Then driving through Tanzania we found ourselves looking at a long stretch of single-track road which dipped into a huge mud bowl at the bottom. The road was reasonably passable, but off line there was no chance – if you went off, you'd never get out.

"We could see a Land Rover approaching and it was clear that we were inevitably going to meet in the mud bowl. John was driving and it was them or us. I looked across at John. He clearly had no intention of stopping.

"I got my head down, the guys in the back got their heads down, we were all waiting for an impact or an off, but we never hit anything. John didn't flinch. As I poked my head up and looked back I saw the Land Rover off the road at a crazy angle and a whole bunch of Tanzanians emerging from it. I've no idea how they got back on the road, but in the circumstances, it didn't seem wise to stop.

"That was pretty frightening, but you couldn't tell John anything, it was just a case of 'Oh Jesus Christ, I wish I wasn't here.'"

The four put the speedo cable back before they returned, but they hadn't reckoned with the wiles of the courier ...

Back to Steve: "We had a persistent problem on the holiday in that our courier was a raving queen [homosexual], as was the hotel manager. We were the only four blokes on their own in the hotel, so some attempts were made at 'contact', and these were not well received. The courier knew where we'd been, because we'd been away for four days, and he knew where we'd hired the car because he'd told us where to get it. On our return he noted the mileage on the clock and told the hire company it must be false.

"The car was absolutely shagged. The exhaust was falling off, both rear dampers had come adrift, yet the recorded mileage was less than a one-way trip to the crater. So the Asians at the hire company did some investigations, found out that we had indeed been logged into the game

reserve at the crater, and then the police arrived and arrested everyone except me – and I was only left alone because I wasn't very well that day."

Things were looking pretty serious until Howard pulled some strings. One of his best friends in London was a Kenyan Asian in the metal business. He had a brother still in Kenya who was already known to the four tourists as he'd invited them round to dinner earlier in their holiday. Now, as a respected local businessman, he was asked to vouch for this renegade bunch of Englishmen.

A scheme was duly cooked up which satisfied honour on all sides. The Kenyan wanted to get some cash to his brother in London, but exchange controls made this difficult. It was agreed, therefore, that a wodge of Kenyan currency would be given to the tourists, easily enough for them to compensate the hire company and buy themselves out of jail, on the understanding that the balance would be delivered to London, with any shortfall being made good from their own resources in the UK.

But the complications weren't quite over. When Steve's dad came to Heathrow to pick up the foursome, he found his son wasn't on the plane. Why? Because to paraphrase Shakespeare, hell hath no fury like a predatory homosexual scorned. The courier had played his final card.

Steve explains. "People in Kenya were pretty poor, so anything we didn't particularly want we gave away – some T-shirts, a radio, that kind of thing. I'd been carrying my ticket in a shirt that I'd decided to give away, so I'd put the ticket in a drawer at the hotel. At the airport I realized that, although I had my passport, the ticket was still in the drawer. The airline was OK about it, as the number was in between those of my travelling companions, but in the departure lounge I was accosted by immigration, in the company of our friendly courier, who told me I had to go and get my ticket. By this time the flight was only 30 minutes from boarding and the hotel was an hour away."

Quite apart from not wanting to miss the flight, Steve wasn't too keen on leaving the terminal in the company of the courier, because as a parting shot, "one of the lads had let the air out of his back tyres. Looking back now, it seems a childish prank, but it was how we felt at the time."

The courier's opinion of his charges, not exactly sky high to start with, was lowered further by this discovery, but eventually inflation was restored, the hotel revisited and the ticket recovered. Steve was then faced with an enforced solo stay in the hotel and, surprise surprise, was asked to 'join' the courier and hotel manager for the evening, in terms which made it clear what was on the agenda. He refused the invitation and the following morning was lucky enough to get his ticket revalidated and find a seat on a flight home, via Entebbe.

NEVER MARRY A MAN WHO DRINKS, OR RUNS A GARAGE

6

As 1975 turned into 1976, the wild, crazy experience that had been East Africa began to recede. Back in the real world, there was a business to be run, racing to be done, and a somewhat complex domestic situation to be considered. Upstairs in the big house on Egerton Road, an ex with two young Chathams to support was now living with a man who was both her lover and John's tenant, while downstairs John was faced with the small matter of finding fresh female company.

He had in fact been tackling the latter problem for some time with his usual vigour, although, to reduce domestic tension, not always on his own premises. And this is where Simcock comes back into the story.

"I had a flat just off Whiteladies Road," Simcock relates, "and John and I spent a lot of time there together, much of it pissed out of our brains. At one point, after the divorce from Sandie, he came round for Christmas drinks and left about three days later. Even before the divorce he would regularly turn up with the most unsuitable women on his arm, sometimes more than one in a day–and they were all staggeringly good looking. Playing the field, that was his life."

Vicky in her 1970s BA uniform.

Unlike John, by 1976 Simcock was involved in a stable relationship with Patti, the woman he would later marry. One day in the flat, John tugged at his beard, a reliable signal that he was about to say something profound, and announced to Patti with a twinkle in his eye and a knowing grin that "I've met this little hostie Patti, bit special she is!" It was their first hint that one woman would eventually rise above all the others.

The 'hostie' was Vicky Kear, an air stewardess who worked long haul for British Airways (BA). And her initial impressions of John were not very favourable, as she explains ...

"I'd been working with BA since I was 24 and I met John when I was 26, in that hot summer of 1976. I'd wanted an MGB roadster, because at the time that was the image, everybody who was anybody had one, lots of hostesses drove them. My father took me to look at this MG, but he didn't look at it thoroughly and I didn't know anything about cars, so I bought it even though it was falling to bits. I drove it on a wing and a prayer, how it used to get up and down to Heathrow I'll never know. Then it finally started letting me down, and my cousin, Andy Kear, who had a Healey and knew John, said, 'I know the perfect

Young Vicky exits one of her father's coaches.

guy to sort your car out, he specializes in sports cars, and I'll take you to meet him. But be careful,' he said tongue in cheek, 'he's an animal.'"

"But if you tell a woman a man is an animal," interjects John with a grin, "often they want to find out!"

So shortly afterwards Vicky Kear, intrigued rather than deterred, turned up at Egerton Road. John's first impressions were definitely positive. "She was rather a nice looking young girl, with a good job and what should have been a nice car. But actually it wasn't very nice at all. In fact I put her B on the ramp and just laughed at it. Apparently I said, 'What a block of crap this is!'"

"He was quite rude about the car," Vicky confirms, "which upset me because I was so fond of it. But he kept the car for repair because I was going away on a trip and I was quite flattered when he said he'd deliver it on my return. 'Oh,' I thought, 'the boss of the garage is going to deliver my car personally, that's good service.'"

Predictably, John was not solely – or even mostly – motivated by a desire to give good customer service. "Little did I realize that delivering the car would mean he couldn't get home, so I'd have to drive him back." And the journey back would, of course, give John the chance to chat up his desirable new customer.

So John delivered the car to Clifton where the Kears lived in a big five-storey Georgian house. "It must have seemed quite grand to John, though in fact we only lived in part of it, the rest was rented out. But it had huge rooms with big high ceilings and, as my mother was a dancer, singer and pianist, we had this huge grand piano in the

entrance to the living room. I remember writing the cheque to John on it.

"My father was one of four boys and his father had a garage in Clifton, quite a big garage in what was then – and now – the most fashionable area of Bristol. They also did coaches, hire cars and wedding cars, so although they weren't wealthy I imagine they were considered quite an important family in the neighbourhood.

"My mother and father met during World War II, when she was 18 and helping behind the bar at her father's pub, the Royal Oak" (which coincidentally is still one of John's favourite watering holes). "The family garage was right opposite and my Dad used to nip across for a drink. As it was the nearest pub to Clifton College public school, which was requisitioned during the war for the use of GIs, it was often full of Americans and my father had to work quite hard to get the message across that the barmaid was already spoken for.

"In the pub, mother saw first-hand what drink could do to people and later, as the wife of a garage proprietor, she experienced first hand the difficulties of the motor trade. She told me, 'never marry a man who drinks, and never marry a man who runs a garage.'"

Three years later, Vicky would find herself marrying a man who did both, but a lot was to happen in between.

The first thing to happen was that the garage proprietor suggested that, instead of going straight back to Egerton Road, they stop off for a drink.

"We did this detour," Vicky recalls, "and stopped at a place called the Dugout, a grimy, dirty, dingy horrible pub whose name conjures up exactly what it was – a dugout underground. But for some reason, John liked it."

"It was a right bloody dive!" he agrees.

"I must say it wasn't love at first sight, though I still felt flattered by the personal service. But then I went away on a ten-day trip to Anchorage and Tokyo, which plays havoc with your time clock, and it was only when I got back that he rang me to ask if I fancied making up a foursome for a day's water-skiing. I was very jet-lagged, but I thought yes, that sounds kind of fun."

John adds: "This was the hot summer of 1976, and Steve Bicknell kept a speedboat at the garage, ready to tow to the lake at South Cerney, near Cirencester. It was only about an hour's drive." In fact John planned to make a weekend of it, but he kept that bit to himself until later.

Vicky continues: "I'd only tried water-skiing once before, when I was an au pair in France, but John just put a life jacket on me and threw me in the water. I'll always remember him saying, 'she popped out of the water like a cork out of a bottle.' I just got up onto the ski and was gone, first pull, away around the lake."

John was very impressed, the more so since his own technique was not exactly elegant.

Steve takes up the story. "We did some water-skiing, then went off for bite to eat somewhere, then just when she thought she was about to be taken home, John drove up to this little bed and breakfast and announced, 'By the way, we're staying overnight!'"

There are two differing accounts of how Vicky reacted to this news. John recalls that "she thought I was being a little forward, but didn't protest too much" whereas Vicky's recollection – undoubtedly more reliable as it was far less influenced by alcohol – is distinctly more robust.

"I wasn't a prude, but at that time I didn't know him very well and I thought it very presumptuous of him to book a room and assume I would stay the night. I thought, 'no, I'm sorry mate, you've brought me up here to have a nice day water-skiing and now you can't get me home because you've had far too much to drink – and you planned on staying anyway! Well you ain't getting anywhere with me.' We shared the room, but I said, 'nope, you can get over there because you're disgusting, you smell of booze, and you've got me up here under false pretences.' He farted and belched all night long."

Steve and his then girlfriend Angie, whose room they had to walk through to reach theirs, had a ringside seat at the opening rounds of this sexual jousting. "She was a bit frightened, to say the least," Steve confirms, "we could see how nervous she was!"

The fact that Vicky had been anything but a pushover served only to increase her allure, and "after that he asked to see me again," she recalls, "but it was difficult because I was away a lot."

To John, Vicky's travelling was part of the attraction because he was, in his own words, "a bit airy-fairy and in no hurry to settle down." He knew Vicky wouldn't constantly be asking, "and where were you tonight?" because she too was happy with a semi-detached relationship – it fitted perfectly with the job she loved.

"It worked quite well," Vicky confirms, "I was gone, I came home, we had good times together and it was fun, then I was gone again and we didn't question what went on when we were apart."

They were realistic about the limitations of their relationship. Neither expected the other to be monogamous. "There's an old – but true! – joke among stewardesses," Vicky relates knowingly, "that if a pilot knocks on your door asking to borrow some toothpaste, make sure you squeeze it through the keyhole."

Vicky fully expected John to make use of this licence. "He always had a lot going on socially, he was frequently invited to be a guest speaker, or to a dinner dance, events

South Cerney 1976, shortly before John and Steve were banned from the lake. A shallow area was reserved for fishermen, but Steve discovered that if you got an old bath, put John inside, hitched it up to a speedboat and drove flat out, you could just get through without grounding. The fishermen were not amused.

where it was natural to want a partner for the evening, and often I was away. Sometimes the evening stayed platonic, sometimes not. Occasionally he took a friend of mine, Stella. At the beginning, we were fairly flippant about it all."

Even though Vicky has never had any interest in motorsport, or speed generally, "life with John was exciting and it was different. But if anyone ever said, 'I bet John won you over with his fancy cars and his way of life,' I'd just laugh. When I first met him, he had an old Granada tow car, which was like a homeless person's car, absolutely filthy. When we first went up to South Cerney for that skiing weekend, I sat in this old beaten up Granada, knee-deep in Coke cans and papers, and the passenger seat was broken, so I couldn't even face him, I had to sit facing the window!

"Later, when I started going to race meetings with him, he'd wake me up at some ungodly hour in the middle of the winter, about 4am, and say, 'for scrutineering we've got to be there at seven,' somewhere way up north, and I'd sit curled up in the back with a blanket over me, freezing cold and miserable, but I'd still go there and be at the side of the track to support him."

Almost without realizing it, the couple gradually grew closer and Vicky came to spend more and more time downstairs at Egerton Road – Sandie and Mike and the children were still upstairs. However, these convoluted domestic arrangements didn't last long. Soon John had the big house to himself, unless Vicky happened to be in town.

"But I had lots of friends. In fact Vicky said when she first met me, 'you know so many waifs and strays!' I remember one night, when Vicky was home from a trip and we were in bed, she said, 'John! There's someone breaking in!'

"'No, never,' I said, and rolled over. But she was right! In the morning we found Chris Harvey, my old journalist mate who did a lot of work for *Autosport*, tucked up in the spare room with some dope-smoking slapper he'd picked up. They'd been at a loose end and Harvey had said, 'I know a bloke in Bristol, let's go there,' so they turned up at my house in the small hours, found an unlocked sash window, climbed in and made themselves comfortable – he knew his way around the house.

"Vicky went ballistic."

Over the next couple of years, a weekend routine gradually developed. Vicky would get into Heathrow about 10pm on a Friday night, it would be midnight before she got back to Bristol and she would go straight to bed, jet-lagged, to emerge around 4pm next day. This meant John could spend lunchtime in the pub with a clear conscience and still have time to cook her a roast dinner and uncork a bottle of red for when she got up.

John grins mischievously. "It seemed to have the desired effect. She thought, 'what a wonderful guy, he makes me such a good meal!'"

He was building up lots of brownie points, but before long he would need every one of them. "I've done this all my life," he muses, "you can stack the tins so high, but you always manage to kick the bottom bugger out."

The signal for the collapse of his carefully constructed metal pyramid was an invitation in 1978 to a wedding on the west coast of Ireland. Tony Fowles, of scaffolding fame, had a brand-new Lotus Esprit, a limited edition in black and gold JPS (John Player Special) colours, and John persuaded Tony to lend it to him for the trip. Naturally, the weekend would not be complete without some female company and, as Vicky was away, the mouse allowed himself to play. Trouble was, he chose another cat to play with, or to be precise a woman called Susan Jones*, attired in a very slinky black and gold catsuit. Susan matched the car perfectly – "they looked fantastic together, I thought I was the 'bee's knees', John chuckles roguishly – but inconspicuous she was not.

The plan was to take the ferry from Holyhead to Dublin, but the weather was very bad and in places the road was flooded. There were times when John was unsure whether the low-slung Lotus would make it through. But once clear of the water, the car ran beautifully – "we were passing loads of cars, the Lotus just wanted to go quickly" – and they arrived in plenty of time for the 3am ferry. At the port there was a huge queue of cars, but John wasn't worried, he was reasonably near the front and had a confirmed booking.

It soon transpired, however, that tonight's sailing would be the first for three days on account of the bad weather. Many people ahead of them had been waiting for days and although the Lotus reached the slipway, the crewman's hand went up as the car in front clanked up the ramp.

John got out and tried to persuade them. "Surely you can move everyone up a bit and get one more on? It's only a little Lotus." It turned out that the crew had already done just that for other drivers, but with the help of a £20 note the ferrymen managed to do it some more, and they were away.

"The ferry was like a cattle boat. There were people sitting on the stairs, you couldn't buy food, it was dreadful. I sussed out that the staff quarters were quite plush, so I put my head round the door and said, 'Look it's pretty horrid out there, would you mind if I came and sat in here with my young lady?' I was welcomed, probably because she was quite attractive, I think she was my passport. So we had a reasonable crossing to Dublin in comfortable seats."

In Dublin another problem reared its head. There was a fuel shortage in the Republic and no one was allowed more than two gallons (9 litres). No way was an Esprit going to get to the west coast on that. "Drive to the North and fill up there," was the suggestion.

"Fortunately I knew a Northern Irish Healey owner, Robert Woodside. He owned a trucking company and had recently bought a Healey. I was doing some work on it and needed to see him anyway, so we drove up to Belfast and stayed in the Ballygally Castle Hotel – not a name you forget easily! – just outside Belfast.

"The following day Robert showed me his collection of cars. It included a brand-new Mercedes SL, which at the time you couldn't get for love nor money, but he'd been pushed to the top of the waiting list because he bought so many Mercedes lorries. When he'd finished with a car – he only ever drove one for a year – he didn't sell it, just laid it up in his barn. He wasn't short of a pound or two."

Refuelled and refreshed, John and Susan then set off for the wedding and the rest of the weekend went without incident – the calm before the storm.

The storm erupted shortly after his return, when Vicky received an anonymous letter. It said simply, "I think you ought to know that a Mr John Chatham was in Northern

---

*Susan Jones is not her real name, which is withheld for reasons of privacy.

Ireland last weekend with a lady called Miss Susan Jones." Clearly, John's combination of high-profile transport and high-profile escort had attracted unwelcome attention.

Vicky received this news with mixed emotions. She was hurt, naturally, but she also knew that the boot could easily have been on the other foot. John's weekend in Ireland was only an extrapolation of the rules they'd both been living by ever since they'd met. The main difference was that this time he'd been rumbled, in a way she was never likely to be because whenever she was at a loose end, she was thousands of miles from home.

She discussed the letter with her mother. The conversation is not recorded, but no one could have blamed Mrs Kear if she'd sighed and reminded her daughter of her marital advice of several years earlier ...

Vicky did not vent her feelings immediately, she was due to fly out soon and was glad of the time to think. By the time she returned, she'd made a decision. "I'd thought, 'wait a minute, it's stupid for us to behave like this, it could stop us having a future together. This is someone I want to have in my life, why let a moment of passion come between us?'

"I need to see you," she told him. It was more of an order than a request.

She tackled John head-on, saying – and John is absolutely certain these were her words – "is it me, or the rest of the world? Make your mind up. What do you intend to do?"

John reacted instinctively – he had no intention of letting her slip away. "I intend to marry you."

Vicky, who had been steeling herself for a break-up, had not expected such an unequivocal response, but once she had recovered from her surprise and delight she answered, "yes."

"Usually when you meet somebody who's had two marriages, they try to avoid commitment, but John was totally the opposite. Not only did he not want to run away, he wanted a big wedding. Usually for a second or third marriage, people say, 'let's go to a registry office, I don't want a fuss,' but John wanted all the pomp and ceremony – the band, the cars, the big reception with hundreds of people. It was great, but I wouldn't have been bothered one way or the other."

His motives are not hard to fathom. He knew he'd been the architect of many of his own problems and he also knew that Vicky was not the kind of woman to tolerate being treated badly. Third time around, John very much wanted marriage to work. A big wedding was his way of telling Vicky, and everyone else, that this time it would be different.

On hearing the news, Steve was filled with admiration for Vicky's bravery. Many years later he summed up his feelings like this: "John's a very easy man to have as a friend, but as a husband ... How she fell in love with him, God only knows, let alone stayed in love with him for over 30 years. She's an amazing woman."

Who wrote the letter? They never found out, though John had his suspicions. "I was going out with a few ladies at that time and I think one of them must have realized Vicky was the person who mattered most to me, and wanted to get rid of her." Paradoxically, this act of jealousy had precisely the opposite effect. The letter forced them to address their relationship and the couple have been solid ever since.

It would be naive, and also untrue, to claim that from that day forth John never looked at another woman – "you can't turn an engine off at full speed, you have to let the revs die down gently" is how he puts it – but there has never been any doubt about where his heart lies.

A wedding day was set for about a year hence, Tuesday 1 October 1979, Christ Church, Clifton.

As the big day drew closer, John began to think about how to spend his last weekend as a single man. There was a hillclimb at Wiscombe Park in Devon that weekend, and John decided that stretching the MGC's legs was as good a way as any to celebrate his last few days of freedom. He didn't often do hillclimbs, but he'd taken the C there some months before and gone quite well, so he fancied another go. Devon was reasonably local, he reasoned, he could easily compete on the Sunday and get back in plenty of time to prepare for the wedding on Tuesday.

"I did the hillclimb and afterwards someone said, 'there's a Healey club meeting the other side of Exmoor, why don't we go?'

"I said, 'OK,' we had nothing much else in mind. So we went to the meet, had too much to drink, and as we were driving back on the Exeter bypass absolutely flat-out in the C at about 145mph (235kph), it threw a fan belt. I stopped to fix it, along with a couple of mates who'd been at the same event. While I had my head under the bonnet, a police car pulled up and asked if we'd seen a car flying past at a high rate of knots. We all looked at each other, everyone shaking their heads vigorously. 'No,' I said innocently, 'we've been broken down here for hours.'

"'Right-o,' said the trusting policeman, and drove off.

"Just as well they didn't breathalyse me."

The wedding day arrived, a grand affair in which cars, naturally, played an important part. John owned a white E-Type at the time, as did a couple of friends, so all the bridesmaids arrived dressed in white riding in a trio of white E-Types, with the tops down. Steve took Vicky to the church in his father's brand-new, silver-blue Silver Shadow,

John and Vicky arrive at the church in a silver-blue Rolls-Royce.

registered 6 EAB, which curiously had acquired a John Chatham Cars sticker.

John had bought a pair of shiny new shoes for the big day, and knew he would be kneeling in front of the altar at one point in the ceremony. As he did so, the ushers had a clear view of the soles, on which John had written a message in large letters. The left shoe said, "HE," the right, "LP." You need a sense of humour to marry John Chatham.

Meanwhile Steve had sneaked out of the church and was engaged in "a little trick." Coincidentally, his father had yet to part with his previous gold Silver Shadow, so as the distance from the church to his father's flat was only a couple of miles across the Clifton suspension bridge, Steve zoomed back to the flat and picked up the gold car, still carrying the same personal plate and already decked with ribbons in readiness for the subterfuge. He arrived back at the church in time for the happy couple to emerge. Neither of them noticed that the Rolls had apparently had a respray during the service, and nor – amazingly – did

anyone else, apart from John's sharp-eyed brother-in-law Martin James.

The couple went to Mexico for their honeymoon and on their return settled back to the kind of matrimonial stability John had not known since childhood. They'd been living in the big house opposite the garage before the wedding, and Vicky's career still took her away a lot, so on the face of it little had changed, but somehow the rules were different now, as was the atmosphere. And John was certainly not complaining.

When Sandie had married John, she'd made it quite plain that she wasn't going to go on living in the same flat that he'd shared with his first wife, Jackie. But when Vicky married John, she knew very well that making a new home together wasn't an option, because the house in Egerton Road was right opposite the garage and integral to the whole operation. John's daily commute consisted of walking across the road.

"It was the ultimate for John, to live so close to the garage," says Vicky. "It was a bone of contention for quite

A Healey was bound to make an appearance at the wedding at some point.

some time that I was in a house which was never of my choosing."

Nevertheless, she made the best of it and threw herself enthusiastically into the unique mix of commerce and friendship that has always characterized John's business affairs. "The kitchen was an extension to the office," she continues, "so anyone who visited the garage – and we regularly had foreign visitors from all over Europe and America – would soon find themselves in the kitchen having coffee and would probably end up staying for dinner too. The house was part home, part office, part B&B, part hotel." In the driveway would be anything up to 12 cars at a time, mostly Big Healeys in various states of disrepair, while at the bottom of the garden was, in Simcock's words, "an unbelievable Pandora's box, although John always knew exactly what he'd got and where it was."

A good idea of how the business operated, and how much it has always relied on John's elephant-like memory for Healey minutiae, can be gleaned from the history of Simcock's 3000 MkIII. He'd acquired it in the early 1970s and John had looked after it practically ever

John and Vicky on honeymoon in Mexico.

On holiday in Hawaii, 1980, John about to have a gliding lesson with "a lovely blonde." He doesn't remember much about the flying ...

since. Each year Simcock, knowing that the Healey was no longer depreciating, allowed himself to spend the money he hadn't lost – in those days about £300pa – on improvements. Gradually the MkIII was brought up to a very good standard.

"Getting it out of John to go on my honeymoon was quite difficult. Deadlines don't always mean a lot, but that one did. He was respraying it on that occasion and it looked brand new, so much so that at the ferry an RAC man said, 'I thought they'd stopped making these?' The passenger door popped open a couple of times, until we adjusted it, but other than that it did about 3000 miles (4800km) without missing a beat – out to the southernmost tip of the Peloponnese via Yugoslavia and back through Italy. I took a spare water pump because that had never been changed – though we never needed it – and a set of front pads, because I knew they wouldn't last the distance – we changed them on the dockside at Igoumenitsa.

"Every time it had anything done it always got the latest Chatham twiddle. Coming home from London flat out on the M4 one night, we pulled into Membury to get

fuel and I heard a horrible noise – we'd hammered number 5 big end into oblivion. John said, 'if you will insist on driving at 130mph (210kph), you need something a bit stronger in the crankshaft area!' So when he rebuilt it he got the crank nitrided. Then we fitted some Chatham pistons and that completely changed the character of the car, it went from plodder to 'revver' overnight.

"But eventually one of them broke a ring, as they were a bit prone to do, and although you could drive it with the tap-tap of a broken ring, you couldn't really sell it. I'd always promised John that he could handle the sale if I ever wanted to part with the car, so when I decided to sell, many years later after 25 years' ownership [I was getting more and more into Astons] I left it with him to fix the engine and find a new owner. It eventually went to Sweden.

"Probably a year afterwards I said, 'I bet you kept the crank out of it,' because I knew he would remember what he'd put into it all those years previously. And he had!"

Along the way, the Simcock Healey also acquired numerous other tweaks. "We went the Cobra wires route early on, with 72-spoke 6½ J (16.5cm) wheels fitted with

75

Michelin XAS 165 15 tyres – technically too small for the wheel, but they gave the effect of a low-profile tyre in the days before such things were available." Stretching the tyre across a wide wheel also helped ensure that it didn't foul the bodywork, though the tyres still stood proud of the front wings. "They threw up a great plume of spray, which made you most unpopular at bus stops – quite illegal, but no one ever seemed to worry about it.

"Another Chatham dodge was the clutch – a combination of Jaguar pressure plate and Land Rover centre plate gave a much more substantial installation than the original Healey fitment."

Hundreds of other Healey enthusiasts can tell similar stories. So how has John generated such customer loyalty?

Every motor trader who cares about his work – indeed every craftsman – is faced with a fundamental dilemma. Few customers have the in-depth knowledge to distinguish between a good job and an excellent one, and fewer still are willing to pay for that difference, not least because the law of diminishing returns applies with a vengeance to any form of car repair. Does the trader work to the best of his ability, or to a workmanlike standard which will ensure him a reasonable living? It's a lucky man indeed who never has to make that compromise.

Despite being by definition an enthusiast market, where the customer is spending out of desire rather than necessity, classic car restoration is not immune to this dilemma. A surprisingly small percentage of owners are genuinely mechanically knowledgeable, while others simply have no eye for detail, or appreciation of it. At the other extreme are the perfectionists who are almost impossible to please. Running a successful restoration business involves understanding your customers as individuals.

Inevitably with old machinery, things frequently do not go according to plan. Unseen horrors are revealed, parts arrive late, and work takes longer than expected. The ability to explain the extras on the bill, while retaining the loyalty of the customer, is crucial.

John Chatham's approach is to sweeten the pill with a blend of bonhomie and hospitality which is uniquely his own – not the contrived friendliness of the double-glazing salesman, but the natural good humour of a man who enjoys his work and loves being around people. You might not like to learn that your ally head conversion cost £450 more than expected because the block turned out to need decking, but by the time you've had several pints in the pub, two hours of hilarious stories, a good home-cooked meal and a bed for the night, you'll write out the cheque with a smile on your face – and come back next year for some new 72-spoke wires.

Organized chaos at Egerton Road in the 1980s, as the American Austin-Healey Club pays a visit.

Customers and family alike universally refer to this invoicing approach as Chatham Added Tax – CAT for short – a term invented by Joe Cox during his spell as John's garage manager. Despite witnessing its application more often than he cares to remember, Joe still shakes his head in wonderment at how John gets away with it. "It's the way it's done," he says admiringly.

The big house opposite the garage was a vital ingredient in this business model. "Although it was a bit ramshackle," admits Vicky, "we always utilized it to its maximum for entertaining. We were party people. On one occasion a contingent of Americans on a motorsport tour of Europe reached the Bristol area and visited us en masse. We blocked off the street, put bunting right across it and the house became an extension to the garage. We had guests queuing in the house for food, collecting their food and going out into the garden to eat, we must have had about 100 people turn up."

By the law of averages Egerton Road, like any residential street, could be expected to house at least one person who objected to the goings on down at the T-junction with Gloucester Road. In the 1970s the Queen's highway had been blocked by an impromptu rubble slide, now in the 1980s it was bunting and hordes of Americans, and day-in day-out there were sports cars being blasted up and down the road. Yet astonishingly, neither Vicky nor John can remember a single altercation with a neighbour.

Most seemed to take the same view as Penny and Tony Macdonald at number 26, who were neither friends nor customers, just ordinary residents. Tony says, "I remember this round-faced bearded man with a rolling gait, tousled hair and a permanent grin on his face. He was always roaring up and down the road in interesting motor cars and no one complained."

"The other residents just got so used to it," Vicky says. "The street was always blocked with John's Healeys, there was always noise going on, and no one ever objected. We always invited the neighbours to join in and our immediate neighbours, Mike and Maureen, were absolutely lovely, even though the 12-car driveway, with its constant comings and goings, was right next to their house. We were very lucky."

John and Vicky had always planned to have a family, but were surprised at how quickly it began, Vicky becoming pregnant in the autumn of 1980, following a boisterous weekend at the previous October Isle of Wight Austin-Healey Club meeting. Soon, John was preparing to become a father for the third time and Vicky a mother for the first.

John says: "For the third birth, I thought I'd better behave myself a bit more. I was around, but I was happy to stay in hovering distance, I didn't think childbirth was a man's job."

When the big day arrived, 16 June 1981, Vicky 'requested his attendance.' John, who had long since learned when to argue with her and when not, and knew from bitter experience that all instructions issued in a maternity room belong firmly in the latter category, went along with it. Playing the dutiful father didn't come naturally, though: "I remember sitting there holding her hand, looking at the ceiling and thinking, 'why on earth am I here?'"

"After the child" – a boy they named Oliver – "was born, I was very conscious of the time. It was a Sunday evening and, in those days, the Bristol pubs closed at 10pm on the Sabbath. It was now half past nine and I was still sitting there holding her hand. But she must have felt my vibrations or something, because as soon as the baby popped out she said, 'you're relieved of your duties, go and get yourself a pint because you need one. I don't need you here any more.'"

This was one instruction with which John was only too happy to comply. Of such understandings are sound marriages made.

After the birth of Oliver, Vicky gave up her career for three years. "With long haul, you have no control over your itinerary, I couldn't go back to flying with a six-month-old baby and be called out for a 21-day trip," she explains. "But once he was at playschool I was really keen to get back and do something, so I worked as ground staff for Danair at Bristol Airport. Then a fabulous job came up at Filton, cabin crew for British Aerospace's daily corporate jet to Toulouse. I did that for four years, but it ended when

A day out for toddler Oliver, trying his hand at a spot of off-roading.

the company got taken over, so then I filled in at Bristol Airport again."

Whenever she could find the time, she'd still go racing with John, but trackside cheerleading wasn't a given any more – motherhood, homemaking, flying and providing the support services for CAT kept her more than busy. Just as Elsie had learned in the 1950s, it was tough going finding time to help run the business, and there was no doubt that John needed help. "Put him with a pile of papers and tell him he's got to balance the books, and he'll panic and run away," she observes.

The pressure increased in 1989, when Vicky gave birth a second time, on 2 May, to a boy they named Jack. Now, with two children to look after, she knew a reliable administrator was essential if John's potentially chaotic enterprise was to be kept in some kind of order.

The solution arrived quite by chance that September, thanks to John's old school friend Philip Parkinson, whose daughter was getting married. At the wedding, the Chathams found themselves drinking with Richard and Christine Maxwell, who had become friendly with the Parkinsons after buying a car from them.

John has never been much interested in pre-war cars, but he did own this fine Aston Martin for a while. Shown here at the wedding of family friend Stein Clarke are John with baby Jack, and next to him Stein's son, James. Behind John is Oliver, next to Oliver is Steve Bicknell's son, Danny, while squeezed next to Danny and almost obscured is James' brother, Peter.

Christine remembers the conversation very well. "I'm so tired," Vicky had complained to John, "you're so disorganized, we really need to get someone to do the paperwork."

Christine continues: "I'd had cancer that year and I'd had a year off. My husband turned to me and said, 'you know honey, it's about time you got out and worked again. You do bookkeeping, maybe you could work for John?' John said nothing, just looked back and forth between us thinking, 'here are these two women, trying to organize me ...'

"At that time, my husband smoked cigars and just at that moment he fancied one. So I leaned across and lit it for him. And although John is not a smoker, he immediately said, 'if you can light a cigar like that, you can come to work on Monday, the job is yours.'"

End of job interview, Chatham-style. It was Christine's first indication that life with John was all about trust and initiative, and not at all about rules and convention.

There was, of course, no formal job description. Her role was to find the administrative gaps and fill them, and she proved so adept at this that she has since become an indispensable part of the business, to the point where she is practically part of the family. More than a bookkeeper, she has also become John's personal assistant, not to mention Vicky's friend. When the Americans took over Egerton Road, she was in the kitchen helping Vicky cook chilli and curry in industrial quantities – "I come from Bermuda and I had a share in a restaurant there." If there was a birthday or anniversary coming up, in John's diary or one of the mechanics', Christine, as the only female on the staff, made sure it didn't get forgotten. Often as not, she was also charged with buying the present.

"Being the only female can have advantages. If I went downstairs and said a rude word, the mechanics knew I was really fed up with them. They didn't realize how important the paperwork was. I wasted a lot of time chasing up invoices they'd left laying around in the car.

"It's interesting working with mechanics because they can be so temperamental. You can do your own thing in

The June 1987 edition of *Supercar Classics* included a feature on
John, with this photo of him in his workshop.
(© *Supercar Classics*)

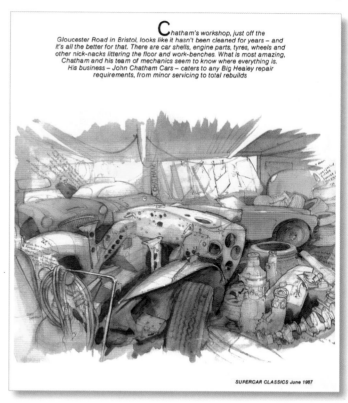

Chatham's workshop, just off the
Gloucester Road in Bristol, looks like it hasn't been cleaned for years – and
it's all the better for that. There are car shells, engine parts, tyres, wheels and
other nick-nacks littering the floor and work-benches. What is most amazing,
Chatham and his team of mechanics seem to know where everything is.
His business – John Chatham Cars – caters to any Big Healey repair
requirements, from minor servicing to total rebuilds

SUPERCAR CLASSICS June 1987

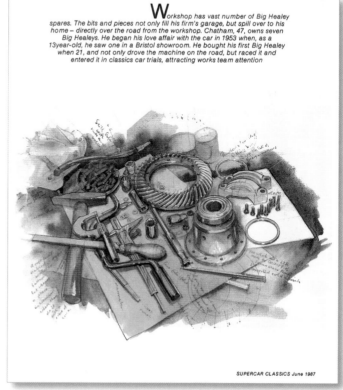

Workshop has vast number of Big Healey
spares. The bits and pieces not only fill his firm's garage, but spill over to his
home – directly over the road from the workshop. Chatham, 47, owns seven
Big Healeys. He began his love affair with the car in 1953 when, as a
13year-old, he saw one in a Bristol showroom. He bought his first Big Healey
when 21, and not only drove the machine on the road, but raced it and
entered it in classics car trials, attracting works team attention

SUPERCAR CLASSICS June 1987

the office, but don't go down to the workshop and move
a tool from A to B, or all hell will break loose. Nick Pride is
like that.

"You have to separate being personal assistant to
John Chatham from being Vicky's friend. And sometimes
it was a thin line. John's a racing driver, a tough rugged
man, and you'd get women looking at him admiringly and
giving him compliments – it happened.

"You work out your relationship with him. He knows I
don't come to work every day, but when the VAT (value
added tax) is due, he knows it will be done. John is a
very good front man and he's got a fabulous memory for
recalling who's paid and who hasn't – and which box he
put some obscure part in 15 years ago. He just needed
someone to organize him."

Two watercolours produced for the feature in *Supercar Classics*.
(© *Supercar Classics*)

FUN RUNS IN THE MOUNTAINS

7

As the 1980s progressed, John found himself drawn more and more into rallying, something he'd had little to do with since the Healey 100 days. The Healey 3000's works career was history, but long-distance events were becoming increasingly popular and many attracted a substantial classic entry. Moreover, in GRX 884D, his beloved 3000 MkIII, he had the ideal car to take advantage of them. A pattern developed where most years he would do one major rally in GRX, plus several shorter racing events in DD and maybe one or two full weekends.

Unlike DD 300, which had pedigree before John bought it, GRX owes all its value to the man from Egerton Garage, for it was never built as a rally car – in fact its pre-Chatham history is completely unremarkable. "It's a 1966 car, originally registered at Abingdon," says John, "hence the Berkshire plates, but the first owner had a rather heavy accident with the car and it was chucked in one corner back at the factory. I bought it as a wreck a little while later, in 1968. I then acquired a brand-new chassis and all the parts from the competition department to create a full works rally car. So the only difference between GRX and the works rally Healeys is the fact that I built it. These days it is probably closer to the original spec than the works cars themselves."

At this point we should mention that, in addition to the damaged original, two quite different cars have carried the chassis number and registration of GRX. The works replica described above has an alloy body and was not completed until 1988, receiving its first outing in the Pirelli Marathon of that year.

From: Steve Norton sales@cape-international.com
the-nortons@uwclub.net
Subject: John Chatham
Date: 11 September 2008 16:45:42 BST
To: nburr@talktalk.net

Hi Norman

I heard you were writing John Chatham's biography and wondered if the following contribution might be useful.

Best regards

Steve Norton

'It was 1988 or thereabouts and I'd just bought my first Austin-Healey. I'll be honest, it wasn't my first choice but I couldn't afford an E-Type Jaguar and 20 years later I'm quietly pleased with the way things turned out. I knew very little about the BT7 MkII I'd bought, so I joined the Austin Healey Club and contacted most of the specialist advertisers in the magazine.

John Chatham was the only 'trader' that really made an impression on me. I visited him at the first opportunity and was not disappointed, John Chatham Cars on Gloucester Road was great, everyone was busy, but in a relaxed way, very welcoming, and the garage was an environment where you could wander about without feeling nosey. John lived just across the road and the ramshackle stores and garages at the bottom of the garden were a treasure trove, on one occasion I needed a small part and was told to grab tools and help myself!

It seemed perfectly natural that John would help with my 3000 restoration and over the following months and years I visited Bristol regularly, so regularly in fact that most Saturdays I'd arrive with arms full of breakfast butties and soon earned the nickname 'Bacon Samy'.

There was always something going on besides the interesting cars. I remember John's son Joe arriving not long after passing his driving test, skidding to a halt in a Cooper S. Another weekend I arrived to see a new BJ8 rally car, it was ticking over on its triple Webers, although the majority of its red bodywork was missing – no bonnet, no doors, just shrouds and wings. John could see that I was impressed and simply said 'take it round the block'. And I did! Typical JC!

What John and I didn't know was that in 1993 I would open my own Austin-Healey parts business and all these years later I thank John for nurturing my interest and unknowingly instilling an appreciation for these cars which continues to make me smile over 20 years later.'

When word got around that John's biography was being written, this turned up ...

But John had decided long before – on acquiring the wreck in fact – that its identity would form the basis of all his rally exploits, so as a stopgap until he got around to creating his works replica, in 1974 he transferred the identity of the

Prescott around 1985, the weekend when the whole paddock was fed defrosted food from the Chathams' freezer, because four-year-old Oliver had been playing with the on-off switch the night before.

wreck to another Healey, with largely fibreglass bodywork, and went rallying in that, until he broke the diff in a fit of over-enthusiasm at a production car trial in 1976. It then mouldered away at the back of John's garden, home to tomcats, mice and whatever other feral creatures were short of a bed, until he struck a deal with Phil Saddington to rebuild and share it in 1978.

When the works replica was finally ready, the fibreglass-panelled car was given back its original identity and sold.

It was the fibreglass car in which John had his closest brush with death, in August 1983 on the Epynt stages in Wales during the Coronation Rally, with Phil Saddington in the co-driver's seat. They were in the closing stages, and well in the lead. "We can practically push it home from here," Phil said, "let's take it easy."

It is always dangerous to suggest this to John Chatham. Especially when, as in this case, a photo journalist had

earlier told him he'd jumped higher than anyone else at Deer's Leap; could he please go a bit higher when the stage was repeated, "so I can get the shot?"

The showman in John could not resist. The flag went down, John's foot went flat to the floor and Phil thought, "Oh shit." Sensing disaster, he snuggled as far down into the footwell as he could. At the jump, John obligingly launched GRX high into the air – really high. "It was a lovely day," Phil recalls, "and all I could see in every direction was blue sky!" GRX veered to the left while airborne, which was unfortunate as the road went right, and rolled end over end several times on landing. It came to rest on its wheels, but with the roll-cage on John's side badly bent, down and forward. John's helmet was split open and Phil, once he had got used to the idea that he was still alive, looked over at John, whose eyes were closed, and shouted frantically "John, John, are you alright?"

There was silence for a moment. Phil feared the worst.

GRX kicks up the dust in the 1983 Coronation Rally. (© Ted Walker)

Then John opened his eyes, thrust both arms in the air and shouted, "Bollocks!" in frustration at having blown a sure-fire win. The car was a twisted mess, far worse under the skin than the photo suggests, but incredibly, Phil was unscathed and John had nothing worse than a sore neck. The St John Ambulance men couldn't believe their eyes.

"The worst thing about it," says John, "was that the journalist was so shocked by how high I went, he didn't get the shot!" Can John remember who he was? "No," grumps John, "if I could he'd be dead by now!"

Austin-Healey Club stalwart Roger Byford happened to be in a caravan nearby and provided a few beers by way of compensation, a process which the pair continued with a vengeance at the nearest hostelry. Then, "completely rat-arsed," in Phil's words, but so relieved at being alive that they just didn't care, they loaded GRX onto the trailer and gingerly trundled home. "Put it out of the way," muttered

"How the hell did we get off so lightly?" A bruised, but lucky John Chatham surveys the wreckage of GRX at Epynt, a few hours after this photo was taken. (© Phil Saddington)

The Coppa was basically an Italian event, but 67 ARX did some sightseeing along the way. (© Nick Howell)

John when they got back to Egerton Road, "before everyone starts to gloat!" So GRX was consigned to Phil's mother-in-law's garage for three months, until the pair summoned up the enthusiasm to take it to pieces. Rebuilt, it appeared in the same event the following year and was subsequently campaigned regularly, usually by Phil.

Meanwhile, the alloy GRX was slowly taking shape. It was not ready, however, by the time entries closed for the Coppa d'Italia of April 1987, a fast all-tarmac event which John very much wanted to drive, not least because it included a stage at Monza, a circuit he'd never tried. So he teamed up with Nick Howell in 67 ARX. "That was an ex-Morley Brothers works car," John explains, "a MkII Healey and one of the first homologated with all the right bits – triple Webers, ally head, it had the lot. I didn't prepare it, that was down to Nick, he always kept it in full works trim and in beautiful condition."

They were part of a five-car team of Big Healeys in that event, joined by Paul Howcroft, George Holt and Ted Worswick, plus American Phil Coombs, who had flown 56 FAC, an ex-Sebring car, to Europe for the event. They were a motley crew, made smarter by red and white team

Four of the five Big Healeys in the 1987 Coppa d'Italia, including three works cars. Left to right, Phil Coombs and Dan Pendergraft with 56 FAC; Nick Howell and John with 67 ARX; George Holt and Jeremy Coulter with 300 HTR; and Ted Worswick and Robert Shaw with 767 KNX. (© Nick Howell)

jackets, courtesy of Paul's clothing company. George had entered thoroughly into the spirit of things and painted his car the same colours, though his use of Dulux and a large brush rather spoiled the effect.

Five Healeys line up in Padua, with Paul Howcroft's 3000 MkII nearest the camera. Shortly after this photo was taken, Paul flew off the road and perched the car in the top of a tree, causing a lot of head-scratching among the rescue crews. (© Nick Howell)

This is what makes classic rallying in Italy so special: competitors gather in Padua. (© Nick Howell)

67 ARX lines up for the circuit stage at Monza. (© Nick Howell)

From a competitive point of view, the Coppa was not particularly successful for John and Nick, the pair dropping out of contention due to a burned-out dynamo, but as with all rallies in Italy, the sheer enthusiasm of the general public made the event unforgettable. Every night the entrants would party in a different town and Vicky flew out to join the festivities.

On one occasion, with Nick at the wheel, they found themselves driving through a town crowded with spectators. "People started booing at us," recalls Nick, "so we wondered if we'd taken a wrong turning – perfectly possible, because John is a bloody awful navigator. But then we thought, 'no, we can't have gone wrong, or there wouldn't be all these people lining the streets.' We were mystified. Then we came to a junction and saw a policeman frantically waving us on, so I gave it a bit of welly and the crowd started cheering! They'd been booing because I was driving too slow!"

John adds: "I drove most of the competitive stages on that event and we had a lot of fun. At one point we found ourselves on a long straight wide road disappearing into the horizon, and in the distance I could see a crowd of people in the middle of nowhere. I said, 'I think there's a checkpoint coming up.'"

"I don't think so," said Nick, consulting the roadbook.

But they had to stop anyway, there were so many people in the road. The crowd surrounded the car. John: "You couldn't see a thing, there were people everywhere, a little old lady gave us a gift of a sewing kit, someone else

gave us biscuits, and a third guy slid up the bonnet with a bottle of wine and a glass. All he kept saying was 'Vino, vino.' So I gave him the thumbs up, he passed the glass through the window, I drank his vino and we went on our way! When we looked back we could see the Italian flag waving again as they stopped the next contestant.

"As we drove away I said to Nick, 'I told you it was a checkpoint!'"

Nick recalls another incident. "We were getting very short of fuel, but it was lunchtime and every garage had a 'chiuso' sign up. Eventually we stopped at this place in the middle of nowhere, it looked just as shut as the others, but we were desperate. Nothing was stirring, complete silence, it seemed deserted apart from a man snoozing in a deck chair, hat over face, Mexican style. But the moment we arrived he leapt up, raced around to the pump and yelled

John Chatham hard at work at Monza, with smoking engine. (© Attualfoto)

out to his wife. She appeared with a baby and a camera, plonked the baby in John's arms and took a photo. Her husband filled us up in double-quick time and then the pair of them frantically waved us off!"

By the following year, 1988, the alloy-bodied GRX was ready to be blooded in competition and John proudly entered it in the first Pirelli Marathon. To his delight, he brought it home second, behind the AC Cobra of John Atkins. "It was won and lost on the long Alpine hillclimbs and the torque and power of the Cobra was always going to win out. But Atkins told me he'd never have gone as quick as he did on the tight stages if it weren't for the reassurance of knowing I was running ahead of him on the road. They were such tight roads and they were open to the public – if you'd met anything coming the other way, you certainly wouldn't have gone any further. With the amount of traffic around by the late 1980s, it wasn't on really, that's why they changed it for later events. One or two of the hillclimb stages were nominally closed, but it's impossible to police such a long road and you'd still find the odd push-bike where you didn't expect it."

The 1988 event was a great success and captured the imagination of classic car enthusiasts worldwide. But in John's view the formula was not yet right: not only had it been dangerously fast, but it was questionable whether Cobras should have been allowed to compete at all, as they weren't rallied in their heyday – for the good reason that their aluminium-panelled space-frame construction would never have stood up to unmade roads.

Quite apart from the appropriateness or otherwise of rallying a Cobra, John reckons he was the moral victor of that first Marathon. "The regs stated that if a stage was completed on time by any car, it was deemed to be a working stage and if for some reason nobody else made it, then your time stood. But in a bit of silly organization on Philip Young's part, they'd decided to end a road section with a check-in at Monza circuit at five o'clock in the evening. That meant you had to flog through the Milan rush hour to get there. As we got nearer and nearer the circuit the traffic got worse and worse, and my navigator Ken Bartram said, 'we'll never make this, it's impossible.'

"I said, 'we're going to.' I went straight across the central

The *Top Gear* helicopter filming GRX on the 1988 Classic Marathon in the Alps.

GRX on a stage near Cortina, 1988 Marathon.

reservation on to the other side of the dual carriageway, headlights ablaze, hand on the horn, heading into the oncoming traffic, got to the traffic lights at the end and, of course, they weren't green for me, but then they weren't red either! So I just wiggled my way round the intersection, shot off left down the road and got to the check-in in time.

"We looked up and down, we couldn't see anything. We were there 10 or 15 minutes and started wondering if we were in the right place, but eventually another car turned up and then the crew for the check-in arrived. They said, 'We know you got here on time because we checked the watches, you passed us going down the wrong side of the road on the dual carriageway, we were stuck too.' But as they hadn't been there to stamp our road book, they decided to cancel the entire stage! We'd have been the only competitors to have got points there, and those extra points would have taken us above John Atkins.

"But that's life."

This disappointment was countered immediately by the next special stage, which consisted of one full lap of the racing circuit from a standing start. "I knew from the previous year that you had to be careful at the chicane and sure enough, when I came to the chicane I was a little wary in negotiating it. But they didn't tell me they'd added a second chicane! I arrived at the second one far too fast, how we didn't slam into the bank I'll never know, but luckily I got through it.

"Then I found that there was a third pseudo-chicane as well, what looked like concrete blocks in the middle of the straight, just far enough apart for a car to go through without a slalom. I came howling down there and I thought, 'they would not put concrete blocks there, they must be polystyrene and put there to frighten us. Well they ain't frightening me.' I went flat between them and I must have missed those blocks by a thousandth of an inch. We did a superb lap, in fact I equalled the Cobra's time on the circuit. And yes, they were polystyrene!"

John didn't always take a support car with him, but on that first Marathon he did, and he wasn't the only competitor who made good use of it.

"It was the end of the day, towards the end of a road section in France. We were nearing a motorway tollbooth,

Lots of silverware on GRX. John has since junked every cup he ever possessed: "I got fed up with polishing them." The car next to it is 274 NTA, a Healey 3000 MkII in rally spec, which Joe Cox was using at the time.

after which it was parc fermé for the night. We had plenty of time in hand because there had been a lot of road stages that day and they'd given us a relaxed schedule in case we hit traffic.

"Roger Byford was following me in another Healey, but I noticed he was dropping back. So I pulled up and my support car stopped as well. Roger said, 'I've got clutch failure, I was just driving along in a straight line when there was a bang and suddenly, no drive.'

"So we towed him to the toll plaza with the support car, jacked the car up and my mechanic and I took the gearbox out. It was difficult to get the clutch out from the clutch cover because it had exploded, all the bits had gone everywhere. And he hadn't built the car that

well because we had difficulty getting the seats out and the gearbox cover off – the screws were all buggered, nothing was done as a rally car should be, to be worked on quickly. But we had the car back on its wheels, running, in 25 minutes.

"Then we had to leave him, because we had to check in before him and we were running short of time, so we left him to bolt the seats in and tidy up. 'Just chuck the seats in and drive it into parc fermé,' I said.

"'I can't bolt them back in there. I'm not allowed to work in parc fermé,' he said.

"'Look, pretend you've lost something under the seat and you've got to take the seats out to find it. Say it's your glasses, anything, just make up a story, for fuck's sake.'

GRX in action at the Mike Spence Historic Rally, a support event for the RAC Rally, on 20 November 1988.

"But he insisted on bolting in the seats at the side of the road. He lost time and didn't make the control. After all our effort, he blew it!"

Fast forward to 1989, and John was gratified to learn that Cobras were to be banned from the event. Now GRX had a real chance of an outright win. Encouraged by the success of the previous year's event, the organizers had encouraged lots of high-profile drivers from the '60s and '70s period to enter, including Stirling Moss in an MGB, Roger Clark in a Lotus Cortina, Paddy Hopkirk in a Mini, Ove Andersson in a Volvo and Timo Makinen in a Healey 3000 – the ex-works car 67 ARX. And they wanted one of the big names to win.

"Having come second in 1988, I expected to be seeded in the top ten. I don't like running first, but I don't like being too far back either, because you're constantly getting held up on stages by slower cars. Nevertheless, even though my record placed me as a top-ten driver, Philip Young seeded me 75, because wanted to give the glory to the ex-works drivers. He reckoned it would be impossible for someone seeded 75 to claw his way up to the front.

"I phoned him up and asked, 'what the hell do you think you're doing?'

"'Trying to make you angry!' he replied.

"'Well you've succeeded.'

"'Anyway, I don't know what you're moaning about, on the third day we reseed everyone. If you're as good as you think you are, you'll be running at the front by the end of the second day.'

"'I've got no chance of achieving that, I've got all

In the 1989 Marathon, John "left Colorado paint on the walls of every hairpin up the Stelvio and you can still see the marks today."
(© Ted Walker)

those cars to get through, to beat on stages, it's a physical impossibility and you bloody know it.' And I seem to recall I called him an arsehole, for good measure."

Whether Philip Young's strategy was really to make John angry, rather than merely shunt him out of the limelight, it had certainly wound him up. John started angry, stayed angry, drove hard and kept driving hard for the whole of the first two days. On the 8.5 mile (13.7km) Stelvio, where the bogey time was set at 16 minutes, John flew up in 13 minutes 17 seconds. As Philip Young puts it, "he left Colorado paint on the walls of every hairpin up the Stelvio and you can still see the marks today." Come reseeding time, John was not only in the top ten, he was number one. The Bristolian had stuck two fingers up at Young in the most telling way possible.

Moreover, he wasn't just in the lead, he was comfortably in the lead. "In my mind, I couldn't be overtaken. All I had to do was keep going."

"I was having an 'animated discussion' about this with my co-driver Ken Bartram, a very good navigator. He was saying, 'keep the pressure on,' and I was saying, 'no need to, we ought to lift off. The roads are very dangerous, high in the mountains, they've got blind corners and we've been driving them too fast.'

"Maybe because of this, I mentally lifted off and when I came to a difficult situation on a very tight left-hander, I drove straight smack head-on into the Armco barrier. The Armco stopped the car, but pushed the steering column back into the car at least six inches (15cm). Both front wheels were facing opposite directions, the radiator had burst and the water had run out, the oil cooler had burst, there was oil everywhere, and the car was a bloody mess. 'That's my rally finished,' I thought.

"There was a service crew on hand to pick up the pieces in support, Bill Price and Den Green, in one of the barges, but when they came across me they took one look, laughed and drove off. I met them later and said to them, 'you pair of buggers, you knew I was stranded and I was in the lead, I was the bloke you should have helped.'

"'But we knew you could fix it,' was the reply. 'Where's the car?'

"'Outside,' I said.

"In the force of the accident, my glasses flew off. Ken, my navigator, was a bit nervous, he knew I was angry. He'd been telling me to go faster and I'd been wanting to go slow, he sensed it was the argument that had caused the problem in the first place.

"'I've got to find my glasses,' I said curtly. 'I don't see without them. You find them.'

"We fished around in the car, no joy. The driver's window was open. I said, 'perhaps they've flown off my face and out of the car.' The car was on the edge of a

"I came to a difficult situation on a very tight left-hander and drove straight smack head-on into the Armco barrier."
(© Jim Watson)

The 1989 Marathon, at the restart in Cortina d'Ampezzo the day after the accident. Ken Bartram (in shorts) sorts out some queries while John waits in a very battered, but now driveable GRX. They were eventually classified as finishing 84th overall.
(© *Old Stager* magazine)

drop, hence the Armco, and the drop was quite sheer. 'They're probably down there, you'd better go and find them, as you caused the bloody problem.'

"So he scrambled down the side of the cliff, which was loose slate, and then shouted back nervously, 'What do they look like?'

"'Why?' I replied, 'how many fucking pairs have you found down there?'

"In fact they weren't there at all. We found them eventually, in the car. They must have shot off my face, bounced off my toes and shot right back under the driver's seat. We had to unfold the seat to get them out.

"Then we set to work. We jacked it up, got the wheel hammer out, and belted the track rod into an S-shape until it pulled the wheel into a position that looked about right. Then we took the oil pipe off the engine, bypassed the cooler and routed the pipe back to the engine. We used pliers to close up the offending cores in the rad, then got water out of a stream and filled the car. I drove it down the mountain to a little garage where we borrowed a rope, tied it round the front and pulled the front back out so the car was driveable. Drove it back to the hotel in Cortina, parked it in the square, and the following morning I decided I would repair it. I was now out of the rally, but I needed a car to drive home – Cortina to Bristol is quite a few miles.

"So, I set to it. I panel-beat the front of the car and put some shape back into it and while I was there the local chief of police, who I'd met the previous year [friendly contact, I hasten to add] turned up. I didn't see him – I'd gone into the workshop to clean my hands – but when I came back out, there was a jug of red wine on the bonnet of the car from the chief of police, 'to improve your carburation.' And this from a man whose English was almost non-existent!

"I got the car half into shape and on the Monday morning I decided I'd go and get the tracking set so I could drive it home without wearing the tyres out in five minutes. I took it to the garage and, again, the guy spoke no English. I tried to explain that I only wanted the wheels to face roughly the right direction. 'No no, car is finished, you can't drive it,' was the reply. He'd measured it and found that the right-hand front wheel was five inches (12.7cm) closer to the back wheel than the left front.

"'Yes, I know,' I said, 'I just want the wheels to face the same way.' Eventually he managed to do what I wanted, but he covered his back by telling me the car was not to be driven. I drove it all the way home.

"It's a talent," he chuckles.

Unusually, John undertook two major rallies in 1989 (and guest drove in a third, as we relate at the end of this chapter). He hadn't planned on a second event, but one day he got a phone call that was too good to refuse. Would he like a free entry for GRX in the Viking Rally in Norway? With free hotel and free shipping?

"What's the catch?" John asked.

"No catch, but you've got to have Anne Hall as your co-driver. And we want her to do some driving." The organizers wanted an ex-works navigator involved to boost the profile of the event.

"Anne Hall was 73 by then, but she was quite a fearless lady. She wasn't used to a car with a twin-plate clutch, it was a bit vicious really, but it didn't faze her, she managed to keep the right-hand pedal on the floor, seemingly all the time. Too much at times! It's quite difficult to slap one of your elders on the wrist for misbehaving, but I had to say, 'Annie, if you don't keep four wheels on the bloody road, I'm going to take the steering wheel off you. You've had two wheels in the ditch many times, when you put all four there, you're out of the seat.'

"She just laughed. She was a good driver – for a woman."

"That was a good event, we enjoyed it and we won the Ladies Cup. The only downside was that we had to buy our own booze, and it was quite expensive. Fortunately, Annie was well aware of this: on the first evening she said, 'John, I've invited one or two to our room, would you like to join us?' and she proceeded to produce a full bottle of gin and some tonics that she'd brought from England. I liked her style!"

In October that year, John was off on his travels again, this time minus Healey as an Italian customer had invited him to guest drive in the Targa Florio Storica, a retrospective event based on the classic road race. Back in 1970 John had competed in the original event in VHY 5H, this time around he would not be driving an MGC, but a MkI Healey 3000, a left-hand drive example he had built up for Beppe Bertipaglia. "I got to know Beppe quite well when I was helping him build the car. He did some of the parts in Italy, I did some here, and eventually he said he was entering the retrospective Targa Florio and would I co-drive with him?

"Somehow, for this whole event, it seemed there was a hand hovering over me, guiding me in some peculiar way. I'd asked Vicky to get me a firm ticket for the flight to Palermo, a stand-by would be no good because a major motorsport event always produces a big demand for seats and Beppe was relying on me arriving on time. But she must have misunderstood me, for the night before the flight, she gave me my ticket and I found out that stand-by was all I had." Apart from warning Beppe that he might have travel problems, there was nothing he could do, but go to Heathrow and hope for the best.

"I checked in at BA, the girl disappeared, then the manager seemed to poke his head around the side of the office. Shortly afterwards she came back out and said, 'It's OK Mr Chatham, I have you a very nice seat.' I was put in first-class and sat next to the actor Peter Cushing all the way to Rome. I didn't know why I'd struck lucky – I'm sure it wasn't the Vicky connection – but I wasn't complaining. Anyway, I expected the real problems to start at Rome, as the aircraft used on the Palermo run were quite small and they were bound to be full. But at Rome all they did was usher me through and give me a boarding pass, I couldn't believe it! Normally they'd point me at the lounge and I'd have to wait until the last second before being called."

A clue that someone might be pulling strings in his favour was provided at Palermo Airport, where John found a car waiting for him. "It was a big black limo with blacked-out windows, and I was whisked off to my hotel, coincidentally the same one I'd used all those years before with the MGC."

"Scrutineering came and went, everything seemed to be going *extremely* smoothly, and then I learned that our entry was actually part of a bigger classic-car team, based at Padua in the north of the country, but funded in large part by a big wheel who lived in Palermo. Their team mainly ran Jaguars, ours was the only Healey.

"I found myself treated like some kind of celebrity. Every evening I was invited out by somebody. On about the third day there, Beppe said, 'tonight, we are going to supper with the Boss, and the Boss has hired a restaurant in the centre of Palermo. But John, please, no jokes about the Mafia, it might be in rather poor taste.'

"In the restaurant, there was one great table laid out in the centre of the room, with about 25 places, plus lots of smaller tables round the outside. When I arrived, a balding gentleman was already sat at the head of the big table. He was well tanned and with white sideburns, and had a classic Sicilian physique: good looking, short, stocky, round-faced. On the right of him were the two biggest guys I have ever seen in my life, presumably his henchmen, they must have been 7ft (2.1m) tall! And on his left were his wife and a lady who, it was explained to me, was his mistress. And next to the mistress was a seat earmarked for John Chatham, with the rest of the table all arranged in order of seniority – drivers at the top, then team managers, then mechanics down the far end.

"Nobody ordered anything. There was no menu, food just appeared. There was wine all around the table, it was there ready. The Boss never touched one drop and never spoke a word. He just pointed – at a waiter, at a henchman, whatever – and things happened. It was quite eerie.

"We hadn't been sat down long before I realized that we were the only ones there. All the smaller tables had emptied: everyone else had gone, vanished."

John's imagination started working overtime. "The curtains were drawn, I thought, 'blimey, I can imagine a shooter poking round the folds of the fabric!' It was a fantastic meal, and a fantastic evening."

At the end of it, the Boss, who had a little broken English, asked John if he'd like to look around his pasta factory, the basement area of which was being used as the garage for the event. "I thought this might be rather interesting, so next morning I arrived as invited. My guide turned out to be one of the henchmen, who did not speak one word of English. But I got the message fairly quickly: he showed me where the trucks arrive – open tipper lorries, which empty their grain into huge gratings in the ground. The whole factory was pneumatically operated: the grain was sucked to the top and was then chopped up and sent down huge chutes to different levels, to be made into various grades of pasta – coarse, fine, dark, white, and so on. At the bottom, when we'd finished the tour, I saw a really dark coloured bag of pasta and joked to myself, 'that's where you end up if you're a bad boy.'"

John felt a little guilty, making stereotypical quips to himself when his hosts had shown him nothing but the greatest courtesy and respect, but the temptation was irresistible. Would he be flavour of the month, he jested privately, if he screwed up on the rally?

"Even though they had some very fast E-Types, they all seemed to think I was a serious force to be reckoned with. All the drivers seemed to want to take me out all the time!

"The classic event was run completely differently from the original in which I'd competed in 1970. The course was exactly the same, but it was not a full-blooded road race. There were stages between the villages, but in each village there was a checkpoint and you could drive as slowly through the built-up areas as you liked – you could have stopped and had a coffee if you wanted!

"Once you were clear of the villages, it was business as usual. The crowd control was as it had always been, ie non-existent! Officially, the roads were closed for the race, but the occasional hay cart still slipped through, just to add a little drama to the proceedings."

Unlike the original race, the retrospective allowed you to take your co-driver in the car with you, though in reality John was at the wheel for all the competitive stages. "But we failed miserably: I came round a bend quite briskly and saw people jumping up and down at the side of the road, and one of them was waving his shirt. It was a yellow shirt and I thought, 'this must be a yellow flag,' but it was a bit too late – an Alfa had blown its engine completely in the

Beppe Bertipaglia driving in the Targa Florio Storica; John was passenger at this juncture. (© Mario Galla)

middle of the bend, the worst possible spot, and dumped oil all over the road. By the time I saw the shirt, the Healey was already on the oil and we had no chance. We slid off rather sharply into a series of horizontal slates, which cut open the left-hand side of the car – my side! – like a tin opener. Not just the bodywork either – it sliced the oil pipe right off the engine, opened up the sump, and rearranged the front suspension."

"You didn't see the yellow?" asked a disappointed Beppe after the retirement. "I saw it, after I'd hit the oil," explained John. Beppe took it on the chin: his attitude didn't change and he remains a good friend. For his part John, although he didn't feel the accident was his – or anybody else's – fault, took the car back to Bristol and repaired it at a very favourable price. "I felt it was the least I could do."

The following year, 1990, John didn't compete in the Marathon because he was involved in the Conclave Challenge, a great event, which we chronicle in the next chapter. But come 1991, having proved in '89 that a Healey was a serious contender for outright honours, he fancied a third crack at what had by this time become a highlight of the classic competition calendar.

He was obviously not the only person to be thinking along these lines, for he got a phone call from Stirling Moss. "He wanted me to build him a rally Healey 3000 for him to use on the 1991 Classic Marathon," John explains.

It goes without saying that John would have been proud to have Moss driving one of his cars, and that it would have done his business no harm either. But he knew Stirling would know this too, and as a result would probably drive a very hard bargain, with no leeway (and certainly no opportunity to levy CAT!). So John, who was in any case extremely busy at the time, politely turned him down. "Stirling," he said, "we've been friends for quite a while and I want to stay that way. I know full well that if I build you a car we're going to fall out. The best advert for my company is me, not you!"

So instead, Stirling got his car prepared elsewhere and they agreed to form a three-car Healey team for the 1991 event. There would be Moss, plus 56 FBC, a 3000 modelled on the Sebring cars and built up by John for Robert Shaw, and a Healey 100 for John and navigator Ken Bartram, OYY 210. "I explained to Stirling, 'I'm going to drive a four-cylinder car, it's not quite as quick as the sixes and' – I joked – 'that might give you a bit of a chance!'

OYY 210 takes shape in John's workshop.

OYY 210 in southern Germany, on the 1991 Marathon, shortly before clutch failure forced its retirement.

"So we had a team of three Healeys, quite a spectacle.

"In fact, my 100 was very nimble and torquey, actually quicker than the sixes for an event like this, though I didn't want to give that away in advance."

But Alec Poole, who was one of the scrutineers at the event, suspected as much. "What are you doing with that?" the canny Irish driver asked John, looking across at his elderly and apparently outclassed car.

"It's just an old Healey 100," John answered innocently, "they're much slower than the 3000s."

"Bullshit. I bet that car's quicker than the bloody lot of them."

"And it proved to be," John grins. On the second timed stage in Belgium only Timo Makinen's Mini Cooper S set a better time. "But unfortunately we had a clutch failure in Germany, which put me out of contention."

The reason it was quick was that OYY 210 was not just "an old Healey 100." Built as a 100S, the rare lightweight version of the 100 with alloy shroud, doors and boot, it was club raced by Mike Wakefield early in its life and had been acquired by John some 20 years before, unfortunately minus its engine. It got used as a donor car for other projects, but John always had it in mind to build it up as the ultimate lightweight competitive 100/4. "The

1991 Britannia Rally, and John Chatham leaves Oulton Park with OYY 210 after rolling it at Donington Park. Fellow competitor Ian Shapland, later to be editor of *Old Stager* magazine, took this shot while waiting to go into the circuit. He recalls thinking uncharitably, "that's another place we've made!" (© *Old Stager* magazine).

long-stroke four has lots of torque which is exactly what you need on an event like the Marathon, particularly for hairpin bends. I wanted to prove that a 100/4 could be quicker than a 3000."

Later that year OYY competed in the International Rally Britannia, a classic supporting rally to the RAC Rally of Great Britain. "I trailered the car to the start of the event and then discovered that all entries had to be taxed and street legal. I wasn't too worried about driving it without road tax – I'd paid so much tax on so many cars over the years that I thought I was due for a bit of light relief – but I had to get through scrutineering, so I whipped the tax disc off my Range Rover and stuck it on the Healey – no one noticed that the registration was wrong. But then I forgot to take it off."

It proved to be one of John's more eventful rallies because at Donington Park, where a stage was formed by using part of the circuit in the reverse direction, he slid off the track at the Craner Curves, the car dug into the gravel and rolled. The hardtop looked very second-hand and the windscreen was shattered, with glass spread all over the trackside, but the roll-bar under the hardtop did its job and, amazingly, John and the long-suffering Ken Bartram escaped unscathed.

They inspected the car. "The accident didn't seem to have misaligned any wheels, so we kept going."

It was desperately cold though. "Driving over the Pennines, the only way we could keep from freezing to

In addition to appearing on the cover of various Austin-Healey and club publications, John's exploits and his cars have reached a wider enthusiast audience on many occasions. In chronological order, front covers include: *Autosport* (21 Feb 1969, see also Chapter 3), *Supercar Classics* (Jun 1987), *Auto Passion* (French, Aug 1987), *Classic Cars* (Sep 1988), *Auto d'Epoca* (Italian, Apr 1989), *Vintage Motorsport* (American, Nov-Dec 1990, see also Chapter 8) and *British Car* (American, Dec 1990). (All covers © their respective publisher)

death was by driving so close behind a lorry that you picked up some heat from it, although of course you also had to suffer the fumes. It was a choice of choke or freeze. But I think I must be the only person to have rolled a Healey in a rally and completed the event." They were eventually classified 62nd out of 88 starters.

A few days later John got a phone call from the marshal at the point where he'd rolled the car. He'd left a couple of things behind at the site of the accident, would he like them posted back? There was a dipstick, which had fallen out when the engine went upside down, and a tax disc, which the marshal had found, still stuck to a shard of glass. "Strangely though," he said, "it doesn't seem to match your registration!"

But he put it in the post anyway.

IT'S CARNAGE OUT THERE

8

In 1986 the ASAVE, the French equivalent of the HSCC (Historic Sports Car Club), agreed with Club Austin-Healey France to make Austin-Healey the featured marque at the following year's Grand Prix de l'Age d'Or, in celebration of the club's tenth anniversary. Club president Henri Maisonneuve and his wife Béatrice asked their British counterparts to help and as a result Joe Cox became involved.

Joe, who was John's garage manager for several years and by this time was also heavily involved with the Austin-Healey Club, suggested running a Big Healey race, something which hadn't happened since the 1960s. He took the organization of the grid under his wing and John Chatham volunteered to get in touch with American Healey racers. To everyone's surprise Phil Coombs and Dan Pendergraft agreed to ship their cars to Europe to compete. International classic Healey racing was born.

The sight of an entire grid of 22 Big Healeys lined up to do battle at the banked circuit of Montlhéry in June 1987 was inspirational and the race was a huge success. John Chatham won, but Phil Coombs finished second and this planted a seed in the Americans' minds. Before long an idea had firmly taken root and they were saying to themselves, "we must do something like this in the US and challenge these guys on our home soil!" And with the help of Dick Lunney of the Austin-Healey Club of America, and a huge number of other companies and individuals too numerous to mention here, that's exactly what they did.

Every year Healey enthusiasts from all over the US gather for an annual conclave, and the plan was to have a race series centred on this event. They called it the

DD on its way to victory at Montlhéry in 1987. (© Joe Cox)

John with the other winners of the 1987 Healey race at Montlhéry: Phil Coombs (centre) was second and Mark Schmidt (right) third. (© Joe Cox)

On the road during the 1987 Montlhéry weekend: Nick (in 67 ARX, still with Coppa d'Italia race panel) talks to John; Phil Coombs on left; French motoring author and Healey expert Hervé Chevalier on right. (© Joe Cox)

Montlhéry 1987: Aided by some franglais and a few hand gestures, John describes the finer points of manhandling DD around the banking to Béatrice Maisonneuve, while Nick Howell looks on. (© Joe Cox)

This splendid oil painting by well known Bristol artist Andrew Burns Colwill shows the 1987 Healey race at Montlhéry, and was created as a publicity aid for the Conclave Challenge. Artistic licence was used as regards the order of the cars – though DD was correctly shown in the lead – in order to put the 'green trio' at the front. The original now hangs on the wall of John's study.

Conclave Challenge, a challenge to which British drivers, including John, responded enthusiastically.

The date proposed was summer 1990, not long after his 50th birthday, and he couldn't think of a better birthday present than to go racing in the US. Recalling that in 1960 BMC had sent a team of three green Healeys to compete at Sebring, and that in DD he had one of the original cars, he persuaded Steve Bicknell and Dave Long to team up with him and recreate the same image exactly 30 years later. Team Healey for the US was born: DD 300, plus Steve's UJJ 677, plus Dave Long's 870 BTV, all in the same classic shade of British Racing Green, but now with white hardtops. DD had already reverted to this colour, following its repaint in a brighter metallic green after its red groundhog days.

Before long, other drivers asked to join in the fun and eventually no less than nine cars carrying the coveted Team Healey stickers were loaded onto the plane, but the heart of the team was the green trio. Among the other six was none other than GRX, which John loaned to Colin Pearcy for the series.

It was a fantastic effort for a wholly amateur competition: an entire team of nine Healeys shipped from Britain to the US for a five-venue series spread over three months. Steve comments: "Of course quite a lot of drivers take classic cars abroad to race. But a nine-car team? For three months? I can't remember anyone else doing that."

John and Steve readily acknowledge that the series simply wouldn't have happened without the commitment of Dave Long and Joe Cox, who worked tirelessly to pull all the strings together in the UK. At the US end, the Challenge became the focus of the A-H summer, with supporting multi-marque races and lots of ancillary events – the hosts spared no expense in their determination to make 1990 a Healey season like no other. This was not just five races, this was a celebration of Healey-dom.

Nevertheless, to John, Steve and Dave, the fastest British Healey pilots, the nub of the event was the challenge, which had started the whole jamboree rolling. They wanted to beat the Americans on their own turf and take home the Conclave Challenge, which was to be awarded on a best-of-five basis, with victory in each event decided on a points system. Everything else – even the partying – was secondary.

There was certainly plenty of partying on offer. "America is a very social place to race," Steve observes. "They put on a lot of nice things to make for an enjoyable weekend for the whole family."

The British team consisted of John, Steve and Dave, plus David Hardy, Colin Pearcy, Roly Nix, Ted Worswick, Mike Windsor and Peter Kuprianoff. Peter is German, but was accepted by everyone as an honorary Brit, in return for taking on the chin the endless ribbing about his nationality. The American team was more fluid, as not every driver could get to every race. The backbone of the team were Phil Coombs, Dan Pendergraft, Richard Mayor and Bob Wilson, but several others came and went, including Tom Colby, Rich Salter, Van Worsdale, Roland Prevost, Jim & Debbie Keck and Paul Tsikuris, not to mention ace Healey tuner Tom Kovacs.

The idea was to run three races over some three and a half weeks – at Mid-Ohio, Blackhawk Farms in Illinois, and Road America in Wisconsin – with the visitors' families joining them for the second event. After Wisconsin the visitors would fly home for a while, leaving their cars to be stored in Milwaukee and until the time came to transport them to Lime Rock in Connecticut, ready for the fourth round about a fortnight later. The final round, at Watkins Glen in New York State, would follow shortly afterwards.

"When you got to a circuit you felt like Nigel Mansell," Steve recalls. "You arrived there to find your cars under an awning by this immaculate green six-car transporter – cleaned, polished, and ready for you. And you'd think, 'this is lovely, where's my lunch?' To us, it was a different race world, a real luxury, we were used to putting them on a trailer at some God-awful hour in the morning, then grinding up to Snetterton in driving rain, with our sandwiches squashed in the toolbox."

No doubt about it, the Americans went racing in style, moreover in beautifully prepared cars, many of which were more powerful than their British rivals. "We took over some of Europe's best cars, but some of the American Healeys were stunning," Steve says.

Team Healey travelling the Atlantic in high spirits, flying first class courtesy of BA.

Conclave Challengers: Ted Worswick (left) and Joe Cox ... (© Joe Cox)

... Dave Hardy ... (© Joe Cox)

... Colin Pearcy in a stressed moment ... (© Joe Cox)

... Dave Long ... (© Joe Cox)

... Phil Coombs and Steve Bicknell ... (© Joe Cox)

... Mike Windsor ... (© Joe Cox)

... Tom Kovacs ... (© Joe Cox)

... Dan Pendergraft ... (© Dan Pendergraft)

... Peter Kuprianoff ... (© Joe Cox)

... Roly Nix ... (© Peter Farmer)

... and John. (© Joe Cox)

In streaming wet conditions at Mid-Ohio, DD and John felt right at home. (© Art Eastman)

"However, they don't necessarily race as hard as we do with historic cars – the front-runners do, but for most participants it's more of a show. But when we were there, it was not a show. They knew all about us, and our reputation as hard racers." The contrast was neatly summarized at the drivers' briefing for the Mid-Ohio meeting, when the clerk of the course explained that, "this is vintage motor racing, we do not overtake around the corners." Nine Brits let out a simultaneous guffaw. It seemed historic racing in America had a rather more gentlemanly ethos than in the UK.

Mid-Ohio is a 2.4 mile (3.9km) course set in rolling hills near Lexington and the Big Healeys got to tackle it twice

that weekend, once in an all-Healey race and once in a broader Group 8 event. With both races affected by rain, the Brits felt right at home, John putting DD on pole for both races despite never having driven at the circuit before. He went on to take the Healey event and was just pipped in the Group 8 race by a very well driven Lotus Super Seven, in pouring rain.

"We were racing so close, he actually left a wheel mark down the side of my car. I went over to him after the race and said, 'How come an American can drive that bloody quick in the wet?' to which he replied, 'because I'm not American!'" It turned out that he was

The core of Team Healey pose with their cars at Blackhawk Farm, (left to right) Steve Bicknell, John, Dave Long. (© Joe Cox)

David Hardy's 3000, easily recognizable by its bubble roof, exhibits some collateral damage at Blackhawk Farms. (© Joe Cox)

Blackhawk Farms and fun and games at the Conclave: model Healeys for racing (including one carrying DD 300, of course) ... (© Joe Cox)

... and the lads putting them to good use. (© Joe Cox)

an Englishman, Dick Faille. The stewards asked John if he wanted to protest about the Lotus hitting his car. His answer was instant, and dismissive. "He didn't hit it, he touched it. This is motor racing!"

What really mattered, of course, was the team result, and that made good reading for the visitors. With John winning and the other Brits performing well, after Ohio the tally stood at UK 1, USA 0. Geoffrey Healey was there as guest of honour and the team was kept busy signing autographs and generally feeling like heroes.

The action now moved to Illinois, to the Blackhawk Farms circuit a few miles north of Rockford, with the teams accommodated at the Clock Tower Resort in the city. Blackhawk Farms was the venue for the annual conclave of the Austin-Healey Club of America, a purely A-H event, the annual high point for Healey enthusiasts nationwide with concours, social functions, sales, etc. It was a perfect place for the sponsors to reap some reward for their generosity: "I'm sure America was good for our sponsors," says Steve. "There are lots more Healeys there than here, and at each venue hundreds would turn up, some of which had been driven 2000 miles (3219km) to get there. Lots of them will have gone home with SC Parts catalogues. Come to think of it, the series didn't do John's business any harm either!"

Quite apart from the racing, the Illinois round was significant in another way, in that it was the birthplace of Healey Driver International (HDI). Sitting round the pool with Joe Cox, David Jeffery of SC Parts, Charles Matthews and Ted Worswick among others, John proposed forming a new centre within the UK Austin-Healey Club, solely to promote, manage and organize races for Big Healeys running to FIA specs. Joe and Charles were tasked with

The birth of HDI – Team Healey and friends around the pool at Rockport: left to right, (lounging) Pam Warren, Dave Long, Dave Hardy, (standing) Jan Hardy, Steve Bicknell, Colin Pearcy, Ted Worswick, Mike Williams' daughters, John with Jack, Vicky, Mike Williams, Dave Jeffery and Maria Jeffery. (© Joe Cox)

Pete Farmer (right) acted as team mechanic for the British cars. Here, he works with John on Roly Nix's car at Blackhawk Farms.
(© Peter Farmer)

setting this up and after a lot of effort got HDI up and running in 1991. In John's words, "Joe still works very hard at it today, completely unpaid."

Steve: "Blackhawk Farms was a short sharp circuit, quite dangerous in a few places, very much a club venue, but enjoyable to drive. My car was still suffering from the misfire that had troubled it in the first race, but John was on the front row alongside Phil Coombs, with me behind." Steve does not know to this day how the grid positions were arranged – certainly the fastest cars were at the front, but whether by practice times or stewards' whim, he's not sure.

The race went well for the UK team, John slipping past Phil at turn one on the second lap and holding him at bay for the rest of the race, and the Brits started feeling confident. It was now 2-0 to Blighty and the team was finding itself the centre of attention for all the right reasons. Moreover, the hospitality was second to none, so by the time the crews and their families set off for the third round at Road America, morale was very high.

Elkhart Lake's Road America was 4.2 miles (6.8km) of fabulous track. The Ferrari garage cured Steve's misfire and everything looked set for a great race. There was a huge grid of no less than 53 cars, this time determined by proper lap times, but since there were two sports racing cars at the front – a Scarab and a Cooper Monaco, which were a full ten seconds ahead of the rest of the field, the Ferrari GTO of Bob Bodin was effectively on pole, with DD lying second. Steve comments: "It was a mismatch, but that weekend there was no other race to put the sports racers in. Anyway, it didn't matter, all our team needed was for John to come in ahead of the other Healeys and the series was in the bag."

Adding to the mix were an Aston, five Jaguars, several Corvettes, and a positive gaggle of Ferraris. It was a very eclectic grid.

The flag dropped. The first long straight – and it was long – seemed "as wide as a motorway" and by the end of it the power of the GTO had taken it clear of John's Healey. But in a fit of hubris, John thought, "I'll have him under braking at the end.

"And what happened? I went in far too fast, far too deep, went straight off, spun and all the quick boys passed me, including Coombsey!"

In the paddock at Blackhawk Farms with Steve Bicknell's car: (left to right) Roly Nix, Steve Bicknell, (kneeling) Pete Ford, John, Dave Long, Dave Hardy, Mike Windsor, Dave Jeffery, Tom Kovacs, Phil Coombs, Bob Kansa and Dan Pendergraft. (© Joe Cox)

Phil Coombs (105) overtaking Dan Pendergraft at Blackhawk Farms. (© Peter Farmer)

John and DD trying to make up for lost time at Road America, after the spin. "And I had passed the Ferrari, he was not catching me!"

"And you nearly collected me along the way," reminds Steve. "After the race I asked you, 'how did you miss me?' and you replied, 'I drove at you, knowing that you wouldn't be there by the time I arrived!'"

This left Phil Coombs in a race-winning position. He had a very strong engine and, in dry conditions with lots of fast straights, there was no way John could get back on terms. But that didn't stop him trying: he set off at a furious pace in what he reckons was one of his best ever drives, and eventually found himself tucked up behind Steve as third Healey, the pair ruthlessly hammering past everyone they could in uncompromising fashion – by lap six they were lapping the DB4.

But John wanted second, not third. "I looked in my mirror at the approach to the last corner," Steve continues, "and I could see John's beard, but not his car, he was that close, and both of us had two wheels on the grass. Cars were dicing two abreast on that last corner and we

overtook five at once – I went to the inside and John dived across to the outside, appalling driving really because I honestly don't think they knew we were there. Must have looked good to the spectators though!"

As a result of these heroics, John and Steve upheld British honour in second and fifth respectively – it would have been second and third, but Steve was unable to hold his tight line on the last corner and spun. No one got near Phil Coombs though, so as a result the tally looked, in Steve's words, "a bit more interesting."

Even as he relates the story, 19 years after the event, Steve's tone is still one of resigned admiration. Half of him clearly applauds John's chutzpah in picking a fight with a Ferrari instead of merely concentrating on the job in hand and beating a red Healey, the other half wishes he hadn't been so stupid. What was that Geoff Healey said about "not being a team player?"

But it was a great event, with a wonderful atmosphere,

well lubricated thanks to sponsorship from Coors' brewery. The high point was the appearance as guest of honour of a cool-looking South American, who turned out to be Juan Manuel Fangio himself. The Master presented the awards, and as Phil Coombs netted the Best Healey Award, his cup really ran over that day.

So when the cars went into storage at Milwaukee, the Americans were only 2-1 down. Suddenly they had everything to play for.

"We flew into Boston," relates Steve, "drove up to Lime Rock in motorhomes and found another short sharp circuit, beautifully laid out. On the Thursday we arrived there was a little bit of practice, Friday was free practice, Saturday was qualifying, Sunday was church and bicycle racing round the circuit, plus a few parties and barbecues – Lime Rock is a very religious area, so we weren't even allowed to start an engine on the Sabbath – and Monday was racing. So we had four or five enjoyable days at a race track, with the focus all on one race."

Just as before, no expense was spared to give the visitors a memorable time. The high point was when toothpaste magnate and Healey enthusiast John Colgate, who had an enormous palatial weekend retreat nearby, invited the drivers to a reception.

Lime Rock was the kind of twisty circuit where handling mattered more than horsepower – "there was one jump where we never lifted at all" – and Steve and John felt right

Roly Nix giving his mount the once-over. (© Peter Farmer)

The first corner at Lime Rock: John pulls across unexpectedly on Steve Bicknell to take the lead, Steve locks up and collects DD. Moments after this photo was taken, the pair spun and the race was lost. (© Art Eastman)

After the spin at Lime Rock, John and Steve enjoying a private duel, first Steve leading ... (© Art Eastman)

at home. In due course they found themselves making up the front row, but for the first time in the series, they were to have a rolling start.

Steve continues the story. "I got pole with John alongside, and John said, in his wisdom, 'we'll go round the first corner together, make sure the Americans don't get past us, and then we'll sort it out.'

"'Oh, all right John,' I said. I believed him!

"But John couldn't wait. As we got to the first corner, John came straight across in front of me to take the lead, and I hit him in the back. I just wasn't expecting it."

The pair are never going to agree about whose fault it was. As far as John is concerned, Steve rammed him up the backside. Steve maintains John left him with nowhere to go. Whatever the truth about this 'racing incident,' the result was that they both spun and although they got going again, recording fastest and second fastest laps respectively, they couldn't get back on terms. The result was a one-two for Coombs and Pendergraft.

So as the two nations entered the fifth race, a score line that could easily have read 4-0, stood at 2-2. John's impetuousness had made for a thrilling finale.

Things were not looking good for the Brits. The final round was at Watkins Glen, a power circuit where the Americans could be expected to do well. "I took one look at it and thought, 'we're in trouble,'" John recalls.

Steve adds: "There was a speed trap at one point of the circuit, which didn't kick in unless you were doing 120mph (193kph). John and I, with 225 and 210 brake respectively, didn't register. Phil Coombs clocked up 138mph (222kph), he said his engine was developing 285 brake and I believe him."

It was no surprise to find that after practice, the Americans were first and second on the grid, with John third.

John recalls: "We'd hired motorhomes to live in, but we didn't like them much, so we rented a log cabin complex from a guy. It had a bar and everything. The owner didn't live there, he just said, 'help yourselves to drinks and put the money in the pot.'"

Knowing what a temptation this would be to John, and desperately wanting to win the race and hence the series, Phil Coombs arranged with a journalist friend, Burt Levy, to "disadvantage" the opposition.

... then John. (© Art Eastman)

"He sent Burt round to get me pissed. Burt's job was to keep me up half the night, but it didn't work. The following morning we got up early – 6.15 it was – and sat on a pontoon on one of the Finger Lakes. Big spots of rain started to fall and I thought, 'this is playing into our hands.' Soon it was bucketing down."

But Phil Coombs had another shot in his locker. He went to the stewards and persuaded them that, because the race was so crucial, he needed more practice in the wet. Could he enter another, earlier, race to get the feel of the wet circuit? In a fit of patriotic fervour, the Americans agreed to his last-minute request.

John continues: "My spies told me what had happened, but I made sure I wasn't around. Instead I sent a friend with a message: 'Tell Coombsey that I'm in the bar with a bottle of champagne celebrating my win – you've got no chance in the wet.'"

John and Steve, as the two fastest British drivers, worked out their plan of campaign. John said, "I've got to beat Coombsey and you've got to beat Pendergraft. If you don't see my car smashed up anywhere, I'm winning. Make sure you beat your man. I'm not going to go off unless he comes off with me."

"That might sound like bluster now," Steve adds, "but it wasn't at the time. That's just how it was."

John continues: "I appeared just in time for the start, purposely waiting until the last minute, got on the grid – it was still very wet, but it had just stopped raining – and said, 'you'd better move out the way because this is my race, a wet race. You Yanks can have the dry races. Just remember that when you come round turn 4 onto the back straight and lose it in the wet, there's nowhere to go. You'll spin and damage both sides of the vehicle, big time.'"

Steve was listening and watching the Americans' reactions. "That really shook them. They didn't like the sound of that at all."

John knew they needed all the psychological advantage they could get because on a drying circuit, the Americans would still have the edge. If he didn't get past quickly, he wouldn't get past at all.

John's bluster must have spooked Dan Pendergraft because come the start, "he moved over and actually waved me by!" This amazed John, but he was not about to argue. "So I'm sat behind Phil Coombs, I'm just psyching him. I knew where I'd have a go at him, at a series of esses. He was driving very well, but he didn't have the wet experience or the close-combat experience. If I had a go at him there, I'd push him off his line and he'd not only be slow on the first corner, but he'd be off line for the next two and slow there as well. It worked: by the time we came out of the third corner I was a long way in front, so much so that he mentally gave up, thinking, 'surely he can't be that much faster than me? It's all over.'

"As the race progressed, the circuit dried and he was

John and Phil Coombs lead a parade lap at Watkins Glen before their final showdown. (© Art Eastman)

catching me, getting quicker and quicker. Had he kept going right from the time that I'd passed him, he would have won it, and with it the series.

"All this chat, you psyche people out, you wind them up to the point where they get nervous and they do things wrong. I've worked these tricks time and time again. It's down to tactics, if you tell them you're that much quicker, that they've no chance in the wet, their head drops. It's all bullshit, but it works."

It certainly worked this time. John beat Phil, Steve came in ahead of Dan and the series was won. "We did it!" Steve says, his pride undimmed by 19 years. "He did it," John corrects him, looking upwards with an evil chortle, "he sent us some rain." John Chatham is not a religious man, but when there is an important race to be won, he's prepared to make an exception.

The scruffy Jeep whose signed bonnet was left in Milwaukee as a memento. (© Joe Cox)

John looks back on the event with great satisfaction and with much fondness for his rivals and hosts. "They were good racing drivers, they were good at car set-up and they were good at engine development, but they weren't used to the wet and they weren't very good in close combat. They didn't realize the sort of competitiveness there is within us. In America I found the mix of drivers quite the opposite to England. Here, 90 per cent of the drivers are flat out and the other 10 per cent are just posing. In America it tends to be the other way round, everything is more relaxed."

Steve concurs: "A lawyer came up to me at Lime Rock and said, 'I've been coming here to watch motor racing for 20 years, but you guys are really at it, this is the first time I've seen real racing, it's carnage out there!'

"We were really proud that a small group of Brits could make such a big impact, including the front cover of *Vintage Motorsport* magazine, the biggest US classic publication. We'd come over from Europe and, as we put it at the time, 'whipped the Americans' arse.'"

A souvenir from the series is still hanging in the Milwaukee garage where the American team was prepared. John explains: "We bought a Jeep when we were over there to transport the Team Healey boys around, it was an awful beat-up thing, but it went alright and we did a lot of miles in it, went to St Louis, to Nashville and lots of other places. We got all the competitors to sign the bonnet – mostly with screwdrivers! – along with any celebrities who turned up at the circuits. At the end we scrapped the car, but salvaged the bonnet; if we could have carried it back, we would have, but it was a bit too big."

Will the Conclave Challenge ever be repeated? John doubts it. "It was tried again a couple of years ago by the Australians, but not on the same grand scale. Unfortunately, I think the 1990 Challenge is likely to remain a one-off."

There was a sting in the tail waiting for the team back in the UK. So lavish and professional had the series been, that the Inland Revenue couldn't believe the participants could possibly have afforded it on their declared incomes. Some jealous individual had tipped off the authorities, or maybe the Revenue had simply noticed the coverage in the Bristol press. The exploits of the city's larger-than-life racer and sports car specialist had been a steady source of copy for the local newspapers ever since the 1960s, so naturally the American trip was well covered.

The drivers never bottomed the origin of the investigation. All they knew was that on their return Steve and John, along with other participants, found themselves subjected to a grilling about what was paid for by whom and how, by tax officials who had clearly spent a great deal of time researching the minutiae of the individuals' lives.

Staff and cars at Egerton Road around 1991, Team Healey banners proudly displayed following the return from the US. Left to right, Joe Chatham, Alan Tice's 3000, paintwork man Dominic Graffagnino, Christine Maxwell, Mike Windsor's 3000, mechanic Julian Tuckwell, GRX, Pete Ford.

But the drivers had an answer for every question: the generosity of the Americans accounted for a lot of the expenditure, and sponsorship made a big difference too. SC Parts, for instance, paid for all the entries and British Airways helped with travel. In fact when the drivers returned for the second set of races, BA was so impressed with their immaculate turnout that it decided to upgrade them from business class to first class, free of charge. "The Revenue woman was absolutely gutted about that, she thought she had me," Steve says with evident satisfaction.

Having got their teeth into the investigation, the investigators had to justify their existence, so they went to town on John's affairs, going back years in an attempt to find evidence of fraud. John spent over £7000 in accountants' fees defending his position, at the end of which he was told he was in the clear apart from an underpayment of £500. It was an unpleasant – and expensive – end to a wonderful experience.

A LOVE AFFAIR
REKINDLED

9

The first love of John Chatham's life was the Healey 100 he lusted after at the age of 12. And as he observes, "you always come back to your first love. I've had a Healey 100 continuously ever since I was 20, but I didn't get back to developing it seriously until 1991, when I got the chance to enter the Carrera Panamericana."

By this time, OYY had quite a few competitive miles under its belt and was as quick as any 100 anywhere. But the Carrera Panamericana opened up new possibilities, because the regulations were very liberal, just as they had been on the original event back in the early 1950s. "I read the rules of the event and it seemed that, as long as when you opened the bonnet the four plugs were roughly where they should be, and the engine was about the same shape as the original, that was good enough."

The original Carrera was run to celebrate the completion of the Mexican section of the Pan-American Highway and ran from southern Mexico to the US border. Then as now, it was hard, fast and dangerous. In the five races from 1950 to 1954, 27 people were killed – the main reason why it was stopped in 1955.

Although the early stages of the 1992 retrospective were to be run in mountainous terrain, the event would be won or lost on the long straight roads further north. "You'd come over a brow and as far as the eye could see the road went straight. And much of the surface was brand new." John knew that, more than any other competition in his driving career, this would be a horsepower event.

"I'd always fancied doing the rally and people said the ideal car for it was a Kurtis – simple, uncompromising and very effective, with lots of power from a big 5-litre V8 – rather like a Lotus 7 on a grand scale. They had top speeds of around 170mph (270kph). I didn't expect to achieve that with a Healey, but I wanted to get as close as I could, and I couldn't do it in a six-cylinder car because under the 1992 regs they were too new to be eligible. So I needed a Healey 100 with a top speed over 150mph (240kph). Quite a tall order."

The key to success, John hoped, would be a unique engine developed from the diesel version of the Healey 100 block. There is an excellent description of this engine in an article by Mick Walsh in the March 1992 edition of *Classic & Sports Car* magazine. Below, John summarizes the thinking behind it:

"The 2.2-litre diesel version of the Austin A70 engine was developed for the FX3 taxi and commercial vehicles. It was basically the same design as the 2.2 petrol unit that the 2.6-litre Healey 100 engine was based on, but it had much bigger castings to take the 22:1 compression and, obviously, no drilling through the centre of the block for a distributor drive. This made for a much stronger block.

"Although the cranks were interchangeable, the petrol crank was a casting whereas the diesel used a block forging, in fact the journals on the diesel crank were so large that you could regrind them to give you practically any stroke you wanted. We ended up with a superb nitrided crank with a shorter stroke, and then bored and linered the block to get back to a similar capacity to the original – 2615 against the standard car's 2660 – but with much higher compression thanks to Sierra Cosworth pistons and special con rods."

When the 100 was still in production, Geoff Healey

Discussing the 'diesel' with Geoff and Margo Healey.

had considered developing the 100S along similar lines, but had never put his ideas to the test. So he took a keen interest in John's project.

"He would come from Warwick all the way to the machine shop at SC Parts Group in Crawley, where we were doing the work. He was responsible for the ideas and designs that went into that car. First time I ran the engine up, it went to 7700 revs and I shut it down because I was scared of damaging it. The monster flywheel was replaced by an aluminium one with a steel insert, and the triplex chain on the front was replaced by a duplex.

"The distributor we ran from the injection pump drive, which meant it was positioned on its side under the dynamo.

The regs didn't allow electronic ignition, but we found that a VW Golf distributor worked very well. Carburetion was a single 55 Weber carb with an alloy head and the camshaft used a similar profile to the late works 3000s."

Lots of time-consuming detail work was needed. The diesel block's stud holes, for instance, didn't line up with the petrol head. The solution involved plugging and redrilling all but two of the holes in the block, the remaining two being persuaded to mate up by some judicious machining of one of SC's replacement 100/4 alloy heads.

The result was a unique engine, generating 200bhp at 6500rpm and capable of propelling a Healey 100/4 to over 150mph (240kph). It was the product of the most comprehensive piece of engineering development John has ever been involved with, and he remains extremely proud of it. "The whole power unit was just superb."

He fitted it in OYY and, as the Austin-Healey Club's annual Isle of Wight meeting was coming up and Geoff Healey was likely to be there, took it along for him to try. "I'd got to know him well during the project and developed a lot of respect for him. He was a man of few words, but if you listened to the ones he said, they made sense.

"I said, 'Geoff, try that car,' and off he went. A while later he came back, got out, stood there looking at the car, puffing his pipe, and said, 'that reminds me very much of the Healey 100 we put the Ferrari 4-cylinder Formula 1 engine in, back in '55. It was a stunning car, but that's as quick.' Coming from him, that was quite a compliment."

This verbatim extract from Mick Walsh's article sums up OYY's early forays:

"At Mallory Park for a Healey Club Championship round John debuted the 'diesel', psyching up arch rival Dave Hardy about his 'secret development engine.' Hardy has been campaigning 100/4s for many years, so holding him off to take second overall first time out was a proud achievement. The heated ten-lap tussle saw the two cars just 1.5 secs apart at the flag. Constant lap times of 48 secs were only 2 secs off Chatham's Mallory best with DD 300.

Receiving life membership of the Austin-Healey Club from Geoff Healey. "They only did it because they were tired of trying to extract the sub!"

"Other highlights of 1991 were the last Healey race of the season at Castle Combe when, in a father and son challenge against the Welch and Hardy clans, Joe Chatham in his first ever race came home sixth with OYY 210. Dad couldn't catch Denis Welch, but Joe headed the other sons to take overall glory for the Chathams."

Readers will have noted a new Chatham in the above text. Joe Chatham, John's eldest son, had just started competitive driving and was already showing real ability. Soon he would get his biggest test of all ...

"At that time I had a customer working in Germany, an Englishman called Jeremy Barras, who also fancied doing the Carrera Panamericana and wanted me to build him a car. So we started from scratch and built him a completely 'new' car, a white-and-blue left-hand drive 100/4. As the development of the 'diesel' was proving expensive and he had finance available through GKN (a large engineering company) the engine ended up being moved to his car. And he agreed to co-drive with Joe."

An entry in the Carrera Panamericana! With a pristine car and a hot engine! For a driver who had only taken the wheel in anger a year earlier! For Joe, it was the opportunity of a lifetime.

So now there were two Chathams in the event. There

Father and son at Castle Combe in 1991, DD for John and OYY for Joe.

was no time or money to build a second 'diesel,' so John slotted the hottest four-cylinder engine he could into OYY – a bored and stroked unit opened up to three litres – and mated it to a high-ratio overdrive to try to keep the revs down and the block in one piece. Trevor Seckel, who'd raced Healeys for many years, was recruited to co-drive, while Joe was despatched to Mexico to get the lie of the land.

Before the start, Joe phoned home to warn John that they would need substantial sump shields, as the roads were much rougher than anticipated. So when John arrived they sought out a local garage – basically a yard with a bench and a vice, plus a piece of corrugated iron for shelter. While the 'mechanico' was sorting out a suitable piece of steel, a police car drove in and the mechanic broke off John's job to remove its instruments. John soon realized that the mechanic was clocking the police car's odometer.

John speaks no Spanish, but a grin and a finger rotated anti-clockwise told the mechanic that John had worked out what he was up to. To John's surprise, the mechanic

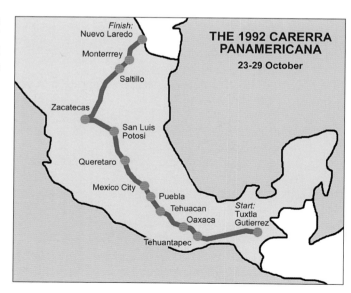

Route of the Carrera Panamericana, a rerun of the famous 1950s road race. (© Norman Burr)

John with Joe on the Carrera Panamericana,
seated next to Jeremy Barras.

responded with a finger rotated clockwise – "he was winding the clock on!" John laughs. "I can only assume the policeman was getting a mileage allowance!"

The event started brilliantly for John. The early stages in the south involved a lot of twisty mountain roads and the Healey, in John's words, "was in absolute heaven. In fact I led my class – over 2-litre sports and racing cars – on days one and two."

Day three provided a very close shave. "I was on one of the long straights doing around 130mph (210kph) when I saw a lad in a field running towards the road to look at the race cars. What I hadn't seen was a donkey in the ditch next to the road. The child frightened the donkey and the donkey jumped out of the ditch and started running across the road. I'd just passed a pickup truck at high speed. I slammed on the anchors and the wheels produced so much smoke that when I looked in the mirror I couldn't see the pickup at all. Next time I looked it had its headlights on! Fortunately I went past the donkey's nose with about a millimetre to spare. If the donkey hadn't stopped, the car would have snapped its legs off, its body would have come across the bonnet and at that speed it would have taken my head off. This was definitely one of the times that I needed the archangel who always seems to sit on my shoulder."

Joe and Jeremy, who were just

The 'diesel' near the start of the Carrera Panamericana.

Joe and Jeremy at the end of their victorious Carrera Panamericana.

behind on the road at the time and saw the whole thing, breathed a sigh of relief. At the end of day three John was still in the lead and Joe was third, with a Corvette sandwiched in between.

Day four proved to be John's undoing. "I was on one of the fast stages when you could look down the road and it went in a straight line, absolutely out of sight. We'd broken the overdrive by then, so we were revving it far too high and eventually the engine blew up."

People often use 'blow up' to describe a relatively minor failure, like a blown head gasket, but this was the real thing. "We never knew what caused it, other than lack of oil in the bottom end. The engine tried to seize, the big end picked up, then the con rod seized and made rather a large hole in the right-hand side of the block. The pushrod on the left-hand side dropped into the sump and was catapulted out of the hole in the other side. That broke the camshaft in half, and that fell into the sump as well.

"It was such an explosion that the aluminium bonnet actually stretched up in a bubble. There were bits scattered all over the road and I was walking up and down collecting them. Later, after I was towed in, we laid all the parts on the bonnet of the car and everyone took photographs"–which unfortunately have since been lost. "I think there was more engine on the bonnet than under it."

Joe, who was running third at this point, stopped to help, but his father frantically waved him on, shouting, "Go on, you can win this!"

And win their class is what Joe and Jeremy did. It was a great achievement for any driver, let alone one of such limited experience, and the memory of the finishing ceremony, with girls lining the road and showering the drivers with flowers, is not likely to leave them in a hurry. Miss Mexico did the honours at the presentation and John said to Joe afterwards, "I think she's taken a shine to you."

Joe was unconvinced, but John's antennae had not failed him. Joe spent the evening with her, chaperoned by her mother, and next morning, as they were getting ready to leave, John grabbed Joe just as he was checking out of his room. "I've just had a call from reception; there's a very nice young lady down there asking for a Mr Chatham. And I think they've called the wrong Chatham! You'd better check back in!" Miss Mexico had come to the hotel, alone this time, to wish Joe bon voyage in the nicest possible way. Dad was jealous!

"It was a superb event all round," John smiles. "You drove like hell all day and partied like hell all night. Every evening you'd stop in a different little village or town and they'd put on a party. In one place we were each given a little jar on a piece of string, to hang round our neck. 'What's this for?' we asked. 'Oh you'll find out, just wear them.'

"Then we started going round the town behind this mariachi band and we found the jars constantly refilled with tequila! At one stage I pointed out to Joe a couple of rather pretty girls waving out of a window and next thing I knew, Joe was standing in the window with his arms round both of them."

OYY after its blow-up.

Every night was party night!

As with many of John's sporting exploits, there is a postscript to this story. After the event the 'diesel' was removed from Jeremy's car and tucked away to await a suitable home. It found one in none other than John's first Healey, SAL 75, which came up for auction a few years back. John fancied reacquiring it himself, but was outbid by a friend of his from Devon.

"The engine obviously wasn't very good because it blew up within a week of his getting the car, so I sold him the 'diesel.' It's detuned slightly, with a lower compression,

Dave Hardy takes the inside line at Mallory Park in 1992 in a neck-and-neck tussle with OYY, which had just returned from the Carrera Panamericana and was still in full rally trim.

but has never been rebuilt and is still in good shape." At the time of writing SAL is right back where it started, at John's place, its bodywork awaiting some TLC (tender loving care) and its owner some CAT.

Will he ever build another 'diesel'? He thinks it unlikely. "It was quite an expensive exercise and quite time-consuming, and there's not a big market for others: people like originality

and there was lots of controversy about the engine at the time, with letters in *Autosport* saying it was all wrong. But the only difference in appearance is that the spark plug leads come from a different place. It achieved what it set out to do and it had a certain legitimacy in that I was only going in the same direction as the factory had considered."

Back in Europe DD, although it was enjoying a more

John in action with Ted Williams' March at Zandvoort.
(© Mark Schmidt)

With Stirling Moss at Silverstone in 1995.

leisurely life than in its glory days of the late '60s, was still being campaigned regularly, though John was starting to offer it to guest drivers instead of driving it himself – for example Ted Williams drove it at the John Gott Memorial Race at Zandvoort in August 1993. It was the Noisy Weekend, organized by the Austin-Healey Owners Club Nederland, and the deal was –inevitably – agreed in the bar the night before. In return for taking DD for the day, John would get to drive Ted's ex Ronnie Peterson March 711 for the day in his first – and as it turned out only – drive in an F1 car. It did not produce a particularly memorable performance, but it did have a beneficial side effect in that it allowed John to tick the BRDC (British Racing Drivers' Club) membership box entitled "single-seat experience."

One month earlier, Gerry Marshall had taken DD to second behind Denis Welch at the Donald Healey Memorial Trophy Race, part of the Brands Hatch Superprix meeting on the international circuit.

Two years later the same trophy was competed for at Silverstone, at the Coys International Historic Festival, and this time Stirling Moss was at the wheel – the only time he has ever driven DD. He qualified fourth, but thanks to a meteoric start, soon got past Steve Bicknell who had started second. Steve, despite having more power than DD at the time, couldn't find a way round the wily GP ace and eventually dropped back, Stirling coming home third.

Part of Stirling's success might have been due to the specially tailored seat, which he likes to fit to every car he races. It wasn't available when DD was trailered to Silverstone, so Christine Maxwell, John's bookkeeper, got asked to bring it later in her XJ6. "I loaded it into the car, drove up to Silverstone and as I was lifting it out I must

have pulled my back. I had to go the medical centre for attention and there were all these men around, wondering why a woman was being asked to 'hump' heavy stuff. I always joke that Stirling Moss put my back out."

Back pain apart, Christine has always enjoyed her role as John's 'Girl Friday.' "It's fun going into the BRDC and being introduced as his PA. I always had to carry his business cards around, organize visits from customers from Europe and take care of all the details. And as my husband Richard is into racing, it rubbed off on me. Just being around a man like John is exciting, he knows so many people."

Meanwhile Joe was continuing to make his mark on the circuits and before long it was common to see two Chatham Healeys entered for a race.

"Montlhéry was always a favourite," says John. "It was a banked oval like Brooklands, in fact Renault used it for testing, but at the time we raced there, only a section of the banking was in use. You couldn't walk at the top of the banking, it was that steep, so you needed to be going quickly to be up there. We used to streak around the top, but to stop you overdoing it they'd put two chicanes in at the bottom. So you were like a dive-bomber, coming off the banking into a chicane and then climbing up again. The chicanes were pretty vicious and the cars used to bottom out.

"In 1995 we took one car for Joe and another for me, and I found myself up behind Denis Welch. His car was going particularly well, but mine had a good top

Silverstone 1995, Moss being chased by Bicknell. (© Mary Harvey)

speed and I could haul him in by the end of the straight. I could have had him on the banking if it weren't for those damned chicanes. I was getting annoyed at this. I could get right on his tail, but then off he'd go again. I thought, 'It's towards the end of the race, I've got no chance of beating him,' so I went straight round the top of the banking, missed the chicanes completely, and came out in front. Of course I got disqualified, but it was worth it just to get my nose in front!"

Most times he got home with good memories, but some meetings he was glad to get away from. John recalls a particularly unpleasant race at the Nordschleife in October 1991, when after driving DD in one event he co-drove Dutch driver Mark Schmidt's Healey MkI in the

Eiffel Classic. No fewer than 125 cars started, in three groups and, "conditions were atrocious, cars were going off all over the place," remembers John.

Mark took first stint and says, "not long after the start Joe Chatham went past me in a 100/4 like I was standing still and I thought, 'you are either unbelievably good, or you are going to spin.' Not long afterwards I saw the car looking very second-hand and Joe sitting despondently on the Armco, where he had to wait for two hours for the race to finish." It was autumn, the temperature was only three degrees celsius and the rain relentless – by the end of the race, Mark remembers, "Joe was shaking, though whether from cold or nicotine starvation I'm not sure!"

Mark wasn't enjoying the conditions at all, but felt

DD leads a gaggle of Healeys into the chicane at the base of the
Montlhéry banking, around 1992. (© Joe Cox)

Montlhéry in the early 1990s: In conversation with (left to right) Trevor Seckel (John's co-driver on the Carrera Panamericana) and Steve Bicknell ...

honour bound to see his stint through. Eventually he came in and told John of the battered 100/4 lying by the track, adding, "I'm glad it's your turn now. It's horrible out there."

As the bent 100/4 was none other than Jeremy Barras' car, which was being given a shakedown prior to its entry in the Carrera Panamericana, John didn't feel inclined to perform any heroics in Mark's car. Taking one unprofitable re-rebuild back to Bristol was bad enough. A couple of other drivers had already given up, and after one lap John

did the same, saying, "we ain't going to get anywhere in these conditions – I'd rather you crashed your car than me. I'm going for a beer!"

Downpours in Germany apart, John enjoyed racing in Europe throughout the 1990s, but the memories of the Carrera Panamericana lingered. Longer tougher events had become increasingly appealing. The excitement of Central America had set the stage for what would turn out to be John's greatest ever challenge, the 1995 London-Mexico.

"YOU HAVEN'T DONE MANY LONG RALLIES, HAVE YOU?"

Early in 1993 Steve Bicknell read about the forthcoming London-Mexico Rally and he was enthralled. "My loves apart from motorsport are travelling and scuba diving, so when I read about the London-Mexico, I said to John, 'That would be fantastic – we could combine all three in one trip. And you've already got the car – GRX.'"

It sounded like a great adventure. Scheduled for 1995 to celebrate the 25th anniversary of the original 1970 London-Mexico, the rally was to run with 42 special stages through 18 countries, all timed to the second. Fifty-nine competitors from 16 countries signed up. The route involved driving from London to an official launch at Wilton House near Salisbury, then through Europe to Lisbon in Portugal, where the cars would be flown to San Paulo in specially racked Antonovs. From there the rally would drive via Brazil, Argentina, Paraguay, Bolivia, Peru and Ecuador to Cartagena in Colombia where a ferry would take them to Panama. At Panama the cars were to be unloaded and the rally would head north via Costa Rica, Nicaragua, Honduras, El Salvador and Guatemala – eventually finishing at Acapulco in Mexico.

It was already three years since the John and Steve double act had led the Conclave Challenge team to victory in the US and the pair were hankering after another adventure together. "We'd done quite a lot of racing," Steve says, "and we were always looking for something different to do.

"So we shook hands on a simple arrangement. Rather than get tied up with lots of accounts and paying cheques to one another, I would pay all the entry fees, which were pretty steep, but I could manage them because stage payments were permitted, while John would pay for everything to do with the preparation of the car. As the entry fees included flights, ferries, hotels, insurance, etc, basically all we would have to do during the trip was feed ourselves and fuel the car."

The pair were going to have to live in the Healey, with two spare wheels and a large fuel tank, plus lots of spares, for a month. Travelling light didn't come into it, this was travelling weightless. The pair restricted their wardrobe to essentials, in John's words – "reversible underpants and socks," prompting event director Nick Brittan to comment at the start that, "you two guys will be the smelliest on the trip in a car that size" – but despite this they still managed to lose half of it before they climbed the Andes. And while everyone loved the look of the Healey, few gave it any chance of surviving long: "too small, too hot, too low," was a common observation, one wag quipping, "you won't get that to clear the start ramp, let alone the Andes."

But John and Steve reckoned they could spring a few surprises. After all, the Healey had been a formidable rally competitor in its day, and not only on tarmac events. "We could have gone really well – if we'd had the right tyres," says Steve.

This remark reveals a point of friction between these two normally very solid team-mates. For John dropped a serious clanger when it came to tyre choice, opting for a low-profile road tyre – 185 60 Avons – instead of an off-road design. In Europe, this proved to be a disadvantage they could live with, but in South America it was a huge handicap. Not until Bolivia did they change the tyres, substituting 195 65 soft-compound Bridgestone Potenzas,

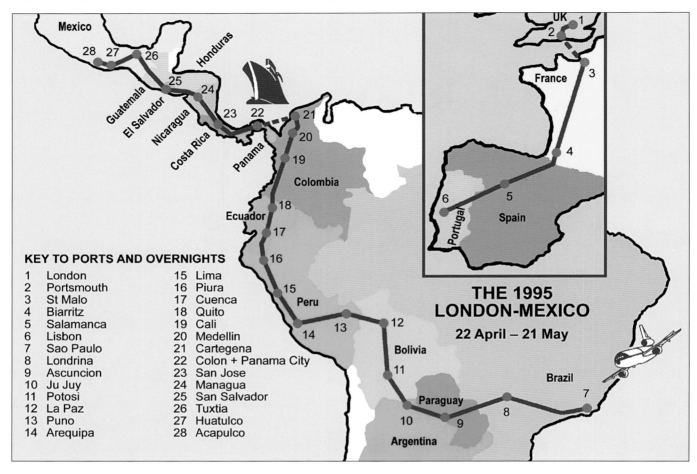

KEY TO PORTS AND OVERNIGHTS

1 London	15 Lima
2 Portsmouth	16 Piura
3 St Malo	17 Cuenca
4 Biarritz	18 Quito
5 Salamanca	19 Cali
6 Lisbon	20 Medellin
7 Sao Paulo	21 Cartegena
8 Londrina	22 Colon + Panama City
9 Ascuncion	23 San Jose
10 Ju Juy	24 Managua
11 Potosi	25 San Salvador
12 La Paz	26 Tuxtia
13 Puno	27 Huatulco
14 Arequipa	28 Acapulco

THE 1995 LONDON-MEXICO
22 April – 21 May

Route of the London-Mexico: 18 countries in 30 days. (© Norman Burr)

The chassis of the GRX being stripped ready for rebuild for the London-Mexico.

And the result. GRX being rebuilt with a full roll-cage in readiness for the London-Mexico.

Jack with GRX en route to scrutineering prior to the London-Mexico.

after which the car was, in Steve's words, "a different ball game, fabulous."

However, it would not be tyre problems that would put an end to their rally, but a whole catalogue of difficulties stemming from one small fuel-system fault. In fact, a conversation John had the night before the event, at the hotel in London where the entrants were quartered, was to prove curiously prophetic.

"I was talking to John Hills, an expatriate Bristolian who had a plastics business in Australia and was competing in a Triumph 2000. I remember it very clearly, he said, with typical Aussie bluntness, 'You haven't done many long rallies have you? I mean long rallies, not these two- or three-day events in Europe, I mean three-week events over the globe. If you've got a problem at the start, it will chase your arse until it fucks it.' And that's exactly what happened to us."

But they had no inkling of any problem as they lined up at the start next morning. Expectations were high: GRX had been allocated running number 7, gratifying as Hannu Mikkola was number 1 and there were lots of other rallying legends taking part, including Roger Clark. It made a pleasant contrast to the manipulations of the 1989 Marathon entry list.

They'd had about a year and a half to get the car built, "but preparation always takes longer than you expect

125

You won't get off the start ramp with that.

One for the album: John and Steve at Wilton House.

and it wasn't really finished until just before we left," John explains. Every cubic inch of the car had to be used and making the most of the space inevitably involved moving things around – the battery, for instance, was relocated low down in the offside front wing, behind a flap.

The biggest change, however, was the switch to an alloy engine. John was uncomfortably aware that the structure of the car was going to take a horrendous pounding and chassis fracture was a serious possibility. By reducing the weight of the car, especially over the nose, the chances of it cracking in half after a huge jump would be greatly reduced. The factory had made a batch of three alloy engines in the competition days, one of which had been scrapped in production (curiously, exactly the same thing that happened later with the seven-bearing MGC alloy blocks). However, John had managed to obtain one of the other two. Developed for rallying and fitted to the very last rally 3000 from Abingdon (now owned by Michael Darcy) it was due to compete in the 1967 RAC Rally. The event was cancelled due to foot and mouth, so the alloy block was never rallied in period and was never FIA-homologated.

John's alloy engine had been tucked away in his 'Aladdin's cave' for years. He'd raced it once or twice in DD and found it made a considerable difference to the balance of the car. Now he hoped that the lightweight engine would help keep GRX together for the toughest rally he'd ever tackled. He wasn't sure if the organizers would

allow it, but he had a simple solution to that problem. "I don't believe I told them," he chuckles, his tongue darting to the side of his mouth.

Another significant change was to switch from Weber to SU carburettors, so that the mixture could be easily adjusted to compensate for the extreme altitudes of the Andes. Taking a leaf out of the SU installation on the Aston Martin DB5, where the jet is lowered to richen the mixture for cold start, John fitted a similar mechanism to the Healey, but with a difference: normal running was jet half up, not jet fully up. This allowed him to not only richen for cold start, but also to weaken for altitude, all from the cockpit. "The theory was perfect," John says, "the execution was perfect, but in the end the switch to SUs was our undoing." For unbeknown to the two Bristolians, there was a tiny hole in the float of one carburettor ...

Leaving Wilton House on the way to ...

... the first competitive stage, held in the grounds of the house.

After the event a commemorative *Book of the London-Mexico Rally* was published, with recollections from each contestant. Here's what John's wrote in it about the early stages of the rally:

"We set off for Wilton on the first stage with the wrong tyres for the deep mud and Steve had already lost the stopwatch. By the time we were over the Channel and into France, I had lost my driving boots. On arrival in Lisbon the Terratrip (odometer) was seriously malfunctioning, the wipers were broken and it was beginning to dawn on us that this was no Sunday outing. We bought a new Terratrip in Lisbon, flew to Sao Paulo, and returned everything to working order with time to spare to visit one or two of Sao Paulo's excellent nightspots! The girls were exceptionally pretty and seriously expensive!"

The early miles in Brazil were encouraging. Day one in South America's largest country took the rally from Sao Paulo to Londrina and included a motorway, which had been specially closed to turn it into a stage. GRX was storming along: the car proved to have an excellent top speed and although temperatures were high and the engine was hot, it was taking the punishment in its stride and John and Steve were feeling good. What they didn't know was that the punctured float had finally sunk low enough to cause the carb to flood. And, as the float chamber drain tubes had been left off in the rush to complete the car, the

In the French Pyrennees following Sandy Dalgarno and Sandy Taylor's Escort.

fuel went over the hot exhaust and ignited dramatically, just as they pulled into the checkpoint.

The timekeepers at the checkpoint – a tollbooth which had been appropriated for the day – shut the doors and legged it in search of a hydrant, while Steve reached into the passenger footwell for the extinguisher. But the catalogue of errors continued. To prevent accidental operation by nosey onlookers, they had anchored the handle with a substantial tie wrap and they'd forgotten to remove it. "I ripped it off with my finger," Steve says, "something you could never do normally, the ties are too strong. I guess it was pure adrenalin. I didn't open the bonnet initially, I didn't want to feed the fire, but I knew where it was coming

The AA on hand at a service point, as it was throughout the event.

from and aimed the extinguisher through the vent." The timekeepers, who by this time had the fire hose working, helped him.

By the time the fire was out, the filter element in the air cleaner had been cooked, as had the capillary tube to the temperature gauge, the throttle cable and some of the other wiring. With the help of the AA (Automobile Association) which was sponsoring the rally and had repairmen on hand, the throttle cable was jury-rigged into action and the wiring subjected to some makeshift repairs, but there was nothing they could do about the air filter, so the engine was now exposed to dust and debris, of which there was no shortage on the unmade roads. Moreover, they could no longer monitor the cooling system.

Later, trying hard on the incredibly rough stage at Ourhinos – on which the Escort of Graham Lorimer and Jenny Brittan overturned – the Healey suffered a puncture. The road was so bad that neither John nor Steve realized they had a puncture until the Minilite was completely

Steve Bicknell looking perplexed on the beach in Portugal.

The tarmac in Lisbon, with competitors waiting to be loaded onto the transport aircraft for Brazil.

destroyed. And when they stopped to inspect it, the car caught fire again, though they dowsed it quicker this time.

They soldiered on, across Brazil, through the flat pampas of Paraguay and into the northern tip of Argentina. Next day – Mayday 1995 – they climbed into the Bolivian Andes, where the roads were so bad that merely keeping the low-slung Healey in one piece was a real achievement. The times became secondary.

"What really sticks in my mind," says Steve, "is that

drive to La Paz, 485km (300 miles) right over the top of the Andes, nearly all of it in first gear over rocks, and then seeing the Pacific the next day. The road was cut into the mountainside, but you wouldn't call it a road really. We hardly ever got into second gear. The Healey had a really hard time that day. It had probably the lowest chassis of any car competing, and we still had low-profile tyres on! We were very proud of that drive."

John adds: "At one point we came round a corner and I said, 'which way does the road go?'

Aftermath of the first fire.

Aftermath of the second fire.

All that was left of the Minilite after driving on a puncture in Brazil.

"'I think it goes that way.'

"So we went that way. After a bit I said, 'this doesn't feel like a road, I think it's a dried-up riverbed,' and it was!"

At 12,000ft (3658m), La Paz is the highest capital in the world and the drive up to it involves a long steep ascent, so it is common for new arrivals to feel the effects of altitude. John and Steve were no exception: they both had terrible headaches, and in John's case his heart was pounding too, so much so that he was sent to bed by the doctor with instructions to rest. The answer was to be found in the foyer of the hotel, where coca tea was available free of charge to all. Made from the coca leaf, Steve describes this as tasting "like a weak Earl Grey tea" and the effect of the cocaine content is to increase oxygen absorption by the blood, exactly what is needed at altitude. Despite its modest cocaine content, the tea is perfectly legal and is widely drunk in South America.

"When you've drunk the tea, the trick is to chew the leaves, then put them inside your gum, leave them there for a few minutes, then spit them out and have another

GRX was a great crowd-puller wherever it went in South America. This is a recreation of a Bolivian publicity poster. (© Norman Burr)

Loading up for the ferry across Lake Titicaca.

On board the ferry.

cup. It really does work," Steve confirms, "after four or five cups the headache went and I felt right as rain."

South America is passionate about motorsport. A police motorcycle escort brought competitors into town and, as the next day was a rest day, the local media had a full day and a half to make the most of their visiting motorsport legends. As far as the Bolivian press was concerned, one man stood out: former F1 ace Clay Regazzoni, who was competing despite being paralysed from the waist down following an accident in 1980. He had a big local following. The newspapers wanted a pretty car to sit alongside their hero and chose none other than GRX. Its British crew didn't know it at the time, but that photo shoot at La Paz was to be the high point of GRX's rally, in every sense.

At La Paz the low-profile tyres were finally ditched in favour of rally tyres, and immediately the car felt much better. On the next day of competition they set off for the highest lake in the world, Lake Titicaca, and the Peruvian border. Crossing the lake involved using ferries, in reality nothing more than small boats powered by an outboard motor and only capable of taking two or three cars at a time. "You drove on over a few planks of wood and prayed that you got to the other side," is how Steve puts it. GRX got across uneventfully, but during the crossing the pair had a good laugh at two less fortunate competitors who were last seen floating off down the lake after their barge's engine failed.

Right next to the jetty on the far side was the start of the next stage, 31 minutes around the perimeter of the lake, on gravel roads with breathtaking drops. The car was going well and spirits were high. John commented

to Steve on the magnificent scenery, only to be advised that, since they had already passed six cars, it might be better if he watched the road.

"Fantastic fun, we enjoyed that," recalls Steve. They spent that night at Puno, on the banks of the lake.

"Then we went up to what was intended to be the highest rally stage in the world at 14,500ft (4420m)." Eventually, this stage was cancelled, officially because the national motor club couldn't provide sufficient medical and security facilities, but also because the ultra-thin air was causing competitors all sorts of problems. Steve recalls wheelchair-bound Regazzoni struggling for breath as he helped co-driver Claude Valion change a wheel, and the cars weren't faring much better.

"The stage started on a hill," Steve recalls, "and Hannu Mikkola couldn't even get off the line, he had to take a run at it. I reckon his BDA must have been down to 60 brake." John managed better, thanks to his novel jet adjustment, but even GRX was seriously down on grunt. He "revved the Healey flat out, let in the clutch and couldn't even get wheelspin."

A long drive across a stony high-altitude desert followed, with a night stop at Arequipa. At a mere 7800ft (2377m), it was virtually at sea level!

Next day the crews drove over 1000km (620 miles) to the Peruvian capital Lima, where they were to stay two nights, the intervening day being occupied by a big loop of three stages, each run twice.

By the time it arrived in Lima GRX was smoking ominously. The dust had started to exact its toll. The last thing it needed was six high-speed stages through what can only be described as a lunar landscape – but that's

In the high Andes. Roger Clark looking pensive.

exactly what it got. Cars were getting stuck in craters full of sand and the only way to keep going in the low-slung Healey was for Steve to shut his eyes and John to weave between the stranded competitors while keeping the hammer down – exactly the technique that had covered West Country trials spectators with mud all those years earlier. But this gung-ho approach did the engine no favours at all – sometimes the sand showered right over the bonnet and, with no air cleaner to speak of, grit was inevitably sucked into the engine.

After a day of this treatment the poor Healey limped back into Lima in dire need of TLC. John recalls: "We stripped it down overnight at the Daewoo dealer and the proprietor Antonio said, 'don't worry, we'll get some new pistons.'

"'How are you going to do that overnight?' I asked, but Antonio was an enthusiast for British cars. The place was fantastic, they seemed to have every imaginable part for every car, or knew where to get it."

Unfortunately the capital's store of C-Series pistons only ran to the +0.030in size, and GRX needed +0.040in, but they did find some new +0.030in rings. So they re-rung the existing pistons after repairing a chip in one of them, and by working late into the night while Steve snoozed on the office sofa, John managed to get GRX ready by the small hours. But during reassembly, tiredness kicked in and he inadvertently bent his trick throttle linkage while putting the head back on, which had the effect of weakening the mixture ...

Time for another extract from the *Book of the London-Mexico Rally*:

"I had planned to charge on through the night, but

was advised against it by our admirable garage proprietor host on account of the hill bandits just north of Lima. He said they paint boulders black and strategically place them on the road at night! We started at first light and sure enough, 100km (62 miles) out, around a turn on the mountain, there were black bounders in position."

Steve was driving, to give the exhausted John a rest. "Steve is not very sensitive to mechanical things," John says with a glance at Steve and a knowing twinkle in his eye, expecting (and inducing) a protest, "so by the time Steve said, 'there's something wrong,' there was something *very* wrong. In fact, just after he said that, the engine died completely and when we looked under the bonnet we realized it had been running horrendously hot – no temperature gauge remember – on account of the weak mixture. We'd actually melted a piston."

With an iron block, maybe something could have been done, but with GRX's special alloy block it was much more serious. The piston seized onto the liner, snapped off the top of the liner and the ensemble then descended into the crankcase, splitting the bore en route and jamming the crank. "Pretty terminal" was how John, in a masterly understatement, described the resulting mess. A formalist might have said it was poetic justice for using an engine of questionable legality in the first place ...

"We flagged down a local truck, got towed into a garage in this one-eyed town in northern Peru, and got the car over a pit – there were no such things as ramps. The friendly mechanico let us use his tools and I got the sump off. I can get most things running, but as soon as I saw inside the engine I knew our rally was over and that we needed a bed for the night.

"The garage proprietor spoke no English at all. We sat down and tried to make knife and fork movements, but in the end the only way we could get through to him was to ring back to the main agent in Lima where we'd rebuilt the engine the night before and get him to explain that we needed food, accommodation and, more than anything else, somewhere safe to put the car. The Healey was on a carnet, secured by the bank for £50,000, and was not insured for theft, so if it had been stolen, not only would we have lost a valuable car, we'd have had to pay £50,000 to the bank!"

Once he understood the priorities, the garage man started coming up with suggestions. He pointed the pair at a local hotel which offered superb food, just as well, as the proprietors spoke no English and the pair couldn't read a word of the menu – "the only thing we could order in Spanish was beer! Evening meal, accommodation and a first-class breakfast was just £34 for the two of us – brilliant.

"But we didn't want to stay forever, so we made

arrangements to get the car to the next Daewoo agent, at Trujillo about 100km (62 miles) away." This had a secure compound with armed guards on the gates. Getting the Healey there was problematic, as there were no breakdown trucks in town, "but the mechanico found a mate with an old American truck which had been converted to diesel and he towed us the whole 100km. It smoked like hell and nearly choked us," remembers John.

Lima, from where the car could be returned to the UK, was another 500 miles (800km) back, so next morning Steve and John left the car at Trujillo and flew back to the capital and the ever-helpful Antonio. With the help of his invaluable network of contacts, he organized return transport for GRX and over the next couple of days also showed the pair a bit of the local nightlife. John and Steve were genuinely grateful, but nevertheless they were under no illusions about the looming bill: GRX was not the only dead rally car in the compound and they knew from other retirees that shipping would cost about $2700, that everything had to be paid up front in cash and that getting large amounts of cash out of the bank was not easy.

But Antonio must have been very fond of British cars, or maybe he just took a shine to the two Bristolians, because he not only offered to do the paperwork for $200, instead of the usual $450, he also kept the towing fee back to Lima to a minimum and suggested that all the shipping fees be paid later, at his London office. However, there was only one boat a month and the next departure was imminent, before he could collect GRX. Was it OK if the Healey reached Britain a month later than the other cars? Having no immediate plans for the car, John readily agreed. He and Steve could hardly believe their luck.

With the loose ends all tied up, the pair were free to enjoy the rest of their holiday and decided to fly to Cartagena in Colombia, where the surviving rally cars were to be loaded on a ferry for the overnight trip to Colon in Panama. When John had failed at Le Mans, he'd wanted nothing more than to get home, but this time he felt more deflated than angry. No one had let them down, they had no one else to blame, they'd simply fallen short. Better to be a spectator than not to participate at all – after all, this was not just motorsport, it was also the holiday of a lifetime.

At Cartagena they tried to persuade the organizers to let them follow the rally in one of the official cars, but that was not allowed; John and Steve thought this rather mean, as all their hotels were already paid for. Nevertheless, they tried to overcome their disappointment by making themselves useful to other competitors, which seemed to be much appreciated. Then they joined everyone on the ferry and, once the cars were off-loaded at Panama, flew to meet the rally at San José, Costa Rica, where they spent a few days lazing around Jaco Beach. Then they flew on again to the finish at Acapulco, where their wives joined them. All this flying and Costa Rican beach life hadn't been part of the plan, but heck, it was a lot more fun than drifting back to England early with their tails between their legs.

They consoled themselves with the thought that the Healey was by no means the only retirement. Only 45 of the 59 starters were classified at the finish in Acapulco, with Hannu Mikkola and Gunnar Palm justifying their number 1 slot by finishing on the top step of the podium.

"Looking back," Steve says, "the thing that stands out to me is that we didn't finish the car in time to test it properly, and didn't go on the right tyres. But we had a fantastic time."

A curious postscript to the trip awaited John when he returned home about a week later. Sitting on his desk in Bristol was a bill of lading from an airline, telling him of a consignment waiting for him at Heathrow. Mystified, he rang the warehouse. "Ah," the warehouseman said, "we've got a nice red Healey on a pallet waiting for you. And by the way, you owe £850 storage charges. It's been here a week."

"What!" exclaimed John. "£850! It was supposed to leave South America in a month's time, on a boat! I've only just flown back myself. I suppose it wouldn't pay me to start swearing and cursing you now, would it?

"The man was very polite about it," John recalls, "but the gist of his reply was that all the time I was arguing, the price was going up! 'I'm only the warehouse manager,' he said, 'I'm not in control of the transport arrangements.'

"We carried on talking light-heartedly, though he could tell I was a little upset. If it cost £850 to store it for a week, what on earth was the bill going to be for airfreighting the thing? It must have arrived only a matter of days after we flew out of Lima."

Eventually John's protests bore fruit and the warehouseman said, "Look, I do like Austin-Healeys, and I'm on night duty tomorrow, starting at midnight. If you'd like to arrive after midnight, you can have the car. No charge."

John couldn't see how he could possibly swing that, but he wasn't going to look a gift horse in the mouth, "so I went hotfoot to Heathrow with a trailer and there it was, still sat on a pallet, with four flat tyres [on account of the altitude change]. I bunged him £50, put it on the trailer, and pissed off.

"I never understood how he squared that with his employer. I can only assume that the guy in Lima paid it

"I was flying." GRX in midair on the Silverstone rallycross course in 1996, before spinning out of contention.

all. I was never charged for paperwork and I was only ever billed for shipping, not airfreight."

The most likely reason for all this was good-natured enthusiasm by a well-connected sports car lover in Peru, but naturally various alternative theories were subsequently aired in the pub, the most popular of which was that the car had been used to hide drugs. However, there was certainly nothing in GRX when John received it. In all probability, he just got lucky – again!

"I've gone through life with a guardian angel," he muses incredulously.

GRX's next significant outing was the Coys International classic meet at Silverstone the following year, 1996. "The

car was still in the London-Mexico trim and we ran a sprint on the figure-of-eight rallycross course. There were lots of ex-works drivers there, the likes of Roger Clark and Tony Pond, and Timo Makinen had a Healey. I made the top-ten run-off and as by that stage Makinen was out, I decided, 'I'm going to bloody win this. I was flying!'"

But it was not to be. He was up against a well-driven Porsche and pushed that bit too hard. "I had the biggest spin imaginable, I nudged the bank, slid down the side of it, and then went right round. I got going again, but it cost me so much time that I was out of contention. To win you've got to stay on the track!"

The same year brought a trip to the Spa Six Hours with

DD meets John Surtees, in the mid-1990s.

The Princess of Wales at a BRDC reception in the mid-1990s,
John lurking in the background.

Ted Worswick and Robert Shaw, the three of them teaming up to drive Robert's 56 FBC – a Chatham-constructed exact replica of the works 3000 MkII, 56 FAC. It proved an enjoyable event, even though it ended frustratingly when the car suffered total ignition failure while John was at the wheel for the third and final stint. The team had been running well up to this point, despite a misfire, which had started during the second stint and got progressively worse. It was eventually traced to the simplest of faults – a dodgy isolator switch.

By now John was in his mid-50s and the hunger to win was waning. He was still running near the front, but his race wins were getting less frequent, as were his race entries. Gradually, his visits to the BRDC clubhouse became largely social, though of course there was still business to be done, Healeys to be built and the right arm to be exercised. He drove DD a few times and went to the Coupe de l'Age d'Or again, but as the decade progressed he racked up fewer and fewer miles in his two principal competition mounts, GRX and DD. It was time for the next generation to take centre stage.

John is so proud of his BRDC membership that he even wears the polo shirt while washing up.

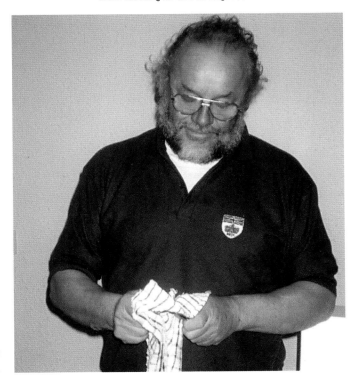

135

Ever the showman, John agreed to be 'gunged' for charity on the Downs in Bristol by Smiley Miley during the Radio 1 Roadshow. Mr Blobby looks on approvingly.

THE NEXT
GENERATION

11

Though he never planned it that way, the London-Mexico proved to be the last major event of John Chatham's driving career. His cheerful 'phizog' was still very much in evidence in the paddock, but increasingly it was as a spectator, with guest drivers at the wheel. After the South American adventure, the events that he remembers most fondly are a guest drive in the Donald Healey Commemorative Race at the 1998 Bathurst 1000 meeting in Australia, and the Austin-Healey Club's week-long internationals – Luxembourg 1999, Switzerland 2004, and Sweden 2008.

The annual Holden-Ford tussle at Bathurst gave John a taste for big V8 saloons, and it is no coincidence that a Holden HSV Type R now sits outside his house (though at the time of writing, that's all it's doing, following some enthusiastic wellying by Oliver).

At the Luxembourg event, John and GRX teamed up again with Anne Hall for a regularity run. "We'd kept in touch over the years and she agreed to be my navigator. The rally started in Luxembourg at our hotel, went to Zandvoort, did a couple of laps of the circuit there and came back. It was all done on average speeds.

"Annie was well into her 80s by then and her brain wasn't as sharp as it had been. At the start of the event

Re-introducing Jack Sears to DD in 2004.

I pulled into the first services on the autoroute for fuel and Annie said, 'Oh, checkpoint? I've got the cards ready ... '

"'No Annie,' I said gently, 'we need petrol.' I realized then that I couldn't rely on her timekeeping, but I also knew that she'd hate to feel she'd let us down.

"So I had a quiet word with Roger Byford, who was

John fixes an oiled plug at the top of the Stelvio after Jack Sears backs off in DD, in deference to heavy snowfall. "It was faster than I remembered it!" said Jack.

supposed to be immediately behind me on the road. I said, 'We're expected to run in front of you, but Annie isn't really up to this. So we'll follow you and check in right behind you every time. If you get everything right, we'll be a minute late at every control, but we'll be happy with that, we just want to complete the event and come back to the hotel with a reasonable result.'

"We did this the whole day. Roger was good enough to wait for us at controls and we clocked in together, me always a minute late because everything was done at one-minute intervals. What he didn't know – I did, but I wasn't about to let on – was that his watch was a minute fast, which made all my times absolutely spot on. We won!

"You know, this is a fluke," John fibbed to him afterwards. But he didn't feel too guilty about the ruse, it seemed like a fair payback for the wasted work in the 1988 Marathon.

The Luxembourg International was also the only time that Vicky has negotiated the Nürburgring, and she certainly has no desire to go again. "I was absolutely panic-stricken, and the thing you never do with John is scream, because the more you scream, the faster he goes. I spent the whole of the Nürburgring sliding down under the dash, begging, and pleading with him – 'please stop, I'm hyperventilating, I'm dying.' All I remember was looking up at his face, seeing him loving every moment of it and hearing him laugh – 'for someone who's dying, you're making an awful lot of noise!' He was clearly having a wonderful time and had no sympathy whatsoever. He

had absolutely no intention of slowing down because as far as he was concerned, I was perfectly safe.

"I can see the funny side of it now. He knows I'm a bit of a drama queen at times. People told me later that I should have sat back and enjoyed the scenery, which apparently is beautiful, but I never saw much of it!"

In truth Vicky, bizarrely for someone married to a racing driver, has never liked speed. "I've never been one to sit in the car and say, 'yeah, go for it John.' I don't doubt his ability, but years earlier he'd taken me round Castle Combe in DD, and it actually took my breath away. After two laps I asked him to take me in."

Highlight of the Swiss International was when DD was finally reunited with Jack Sears, who drove it with Peter Riley at Sebring and Le Mans when it was the works car UJB 143. Jack says: "Because of my association with the car, I always took a particular interest in John's progress and quite often went to say hello in the paddock. I'll always be grateful for being given the chance to drive it again." He kept it for a complete day, retracing a number of famous roads including the Stelvio, where it was snowing hard at the top despite the event being held in late August. In deference to the conditions, Jack backed off, only to have DD do what DD often did when it was not being raced 'at full chat' – oil a plug. John was soon on hand to brave the elements and get his beloved racer back onto all six. "It was faster than I remembered it!" Jack adds.

The male offspring of the Chatham family – Joe, Oliver and Jack – fully understand the appeal of getting cold and oily on top of a mountain, but this seemingly congenital obsession with cars has not afflicted John's daughter Charlotte. As the last decade of the 20th century progressed, Charlotte, born in 1969 and the eldest of the four, was making a career as a hairdresser and has continued to pursue an independent path. She is now happily partnered and the mother of two children.

Joe, just a year younger, proved to be a chip off the old block right from the word go. Simcock recalls: "I remember Joe on the forecourt at Egerton Road – he must have been about four at the time – and Chatham saying to him, 'What car's that?'

"And this little lad proudly looked up at his dad and said, 'It's an Austin-Healey, Dad,' to which he got a playful clip across the ear and his father said, 'Of course it's an Austin-Healey, what sort of Austin-Healey?'

'A 3000 MkIII Dad.'

'That's better.'"

Like Charlotte, Joe was brought up by Sandie, but he spent quite a lot of time with his father, the garage becoming something of a second home. When he left school at 18 with no particular career in mind, it seemed

The opening of John Chatham Cars Ltd, with Simon Taylor presiding.

Guests gather at the opening of Avonmouth.

natural, both to him and to John, to involve him in the business. So, just as his own father had done with him at a similar age, John put him on the payroll. It had worked once and it could work again.

It was an exciting time for Joe. In 1989 the classic car boom was in full swing in Britain and there was good business to be had importing and restoring rust-free American cars. No sooner had he joined the payroll than Joe found himself despatched to the US to scout for suitable machinery. Joe proved so adept at this that what was intended initially as a short trip, with accommodation provided by none other than Dan Pendergraft of Conclave fame, turned into an eight-month stint which took Joe all over the US in a yellow TR6 that he acquired Stateside.

When Joe returned to the UK towards the end of 1989 the boom was peaking, but there was still plenty of work to be done on the cars he had sourced. Within a few months it would be John's turn to focus his attention across the pond, as it was now 1990 and the Conclave Challenge was unfolding. While John was away, Joe and garage manager Pete Ford held the fort.

By the time he was 26, Joe had worked at Egerton Road for eight years and John for 40. John was now 56, too young to retire, but old enough to fancy working less hard and letting the younger generation have their head.

Joe loved the idea and before long the plans for John to take a back seat had turned into a fully fledged project and acquired a momentum of their own. A new company, John Chatham Cars Ltd, would be set up with three shareholders – Joe Chatham, Pete Ford and Bill Sweetnam – and four directors – the shareholders plus John, who was retained as a consultant. Joe would buy his shares courtesy of a partial IOU to his dad and would run

the business day-to-day along with Pete, who was John's garage manager at the time. Bill, who coincidentally would later become a commercial pilot and find himself flying with Vicky, was tasked with funding the operation.

And a lot of funding was needed, for the plans were ambitious. Against the advice of John, the new team decided to abandon everyday garage work and concentrate entirely on the classic market. Moreover, they felt they needed bigger premises to do it from, and rented an industrial unit in Avonmouth, near Bristol.

February 1996 was a heady time at Avonmouth. A big launch party was organized, with lots of motorsport personalities in attendance, including Whizzo Williams, Norman Grimshaw, Gerry Marshall (never one to miss out on a drink) and Simon Taylor, who acted as master of ceremonies.

Almost immediately, it became clear that the business model was not sound. Overheads of the big new premises were too large and the wages bill was too high – there were now four directors to support instead of just John. To make matters worse, the timing was all wrong. By 1996 the classic car boom had well and truly ended and there were lots of cars on the market at prices below restoration cost.

Joe and Pete lacked the managerial training to appreciate these dangers. Had John insisted on Joe going to business school, or spending a few years working for another company, Joe and his fellow shareholders might have been more cautious. As it was, John gave them their head, reasoning that his eldest son had already proved himself to be an astute trader and could pick up other business skills as he went along, just as his father had done. John underestimated how much the business environment had changed in the intervening quarter century.

There was certainly no lack of enthusiasm at

Joe (left) and Pete Ford in the office at Avonmouth.

Avonmouth, or of sporting credibility. Joe had proved to be a formidable competitor – every bit as quick as his father, in John's opinion – and off track the Chatham dedication could shine as brightly as ever. Simcock recalls a trip to Belgium when he had a problem with his car and Joe "went out of his way to help, although he didn't really know me that well. I couldn't speak too highly of him. John, of course, was already down the pub!"

But when it came to the everyday running of the company, being friendly and personable was no substitute for experience and training. And Joe had never built up the depth of mechanical knowledge that comes from the hard graft of fixing cars year-in and year-out. John was ready and willing to fill those gaps, but frustratingly, felt himself kept at arm's length by younger men who thought they knew better. Moreover, basic operational tasks were not getting done. At one point, bookkeeper Christine Maxwell recalls, the premises were freezing cold because neither Joe nor Pete had remembered to order any heating oil. Bill passed round a bottle of scotch to warm everyone up, but this was hardly the stuff of which business empires are built.

Looking back, Joe wishes he'd had more support from his father, but John still had his hands full back at Egerton Road, with what seemed like a thousand loose ends to tie up. He had a fairly modern MoT station, some older workshops, a forecourt and a car lot to dispose of. Not to mention a house, because Vicky, realizing that the changes at Egerton Road Garage represented a watershed in their lives whether or not the Avonmouth venture succeeded, started looking around for a new home as soon as the reorganization was agreed. She'd taken on the Egerton

Road house in a positive spirit, albeit reluctantly. Now was her chance to make the new home with John that she'd always wanted. Nineteen ninety-six was turning out to be as momentous a year as 1970.

"You don't need to live here any more," she told John when Avonmouth was set up. "You could work from anywhere. With your name, the work will follow you."

Initially, John was unconvinced – he'd never thought of himself as a brand. But as events at Avonmouth unfolded and it became clear that his services were likely to be used less than expected, he decided he might as well restart doing what he knew best – repairing, restoring and modifying Big Healeys. Thanks to the combination of Vicky's salary and the capital soon to be released from Egerton Road, he only needed to operate in a very small way – nothing that could be considered a rival to Avonmouth. Just the odd job here and there.

Egerton Road Garage was split into two parts. John retained ownership of the MoT station and to this day continues to rent out the premises, the current occupant being DCL Motors.

The rest of the site he decided to sell, which proved quite complex and needed a bit of professional help. In true Chatham style, the help came from a Healey enthusiast, in this case racer Dave Long, wearing his professional hat instead of his crash helmet. Steve Bicknell had long since moved off the car lot, back in 1988, but since then it had been used by two other dealers, one of whom was still on site. It was decided to give the dealer notice, bundle the car lot with the other buildings and the redundant forecourt (petrol sales having already been abandoned as unprofitable) and then sell the whole package for redevelopment. Ironically, a booze supermarket was built on it.

Vicky's search for her dream home ended with Wellinghouse Farm in Hallen, a 16th century listed farmhouse with plenty of outbuildings for John to play in. It was – and is, for they still live and work there – a beautiful spot. The family moved there in April 1997 and took their by-now legendary hospitality with them.

After the move, with John gradually easing himself back into business, Christine found herself doing the books for two sports car enterprises. Despite drawing on all her reserves of tact and professionalism to avoid being, or even appearing to be, partisan to one venture or the other, she found her loyalty questioned as the company's struggles intensified. She counts this as the low point in her 20-year relationship with the Chatham family.

As the financial screw tightened at Avonmouth, corners were cut, promises were broken and John, whose name was still proudly emblazoned over the door, felt powerless to influence events – he was just one director out of four and held no shares. In little over a year and a half, the company was forced to relocate to cheaper premises, a farm at Westerleigh where the outbuildings already housed some motor trade businesses and had room for another. But that move, in December 1997, only delayed the inevitable and by 1999 it was all over. John Chatham Cars Ltd was bankrupt.

It was a tough time for the whole family, and its employees. Harsh words were exchanged and everyone came out of it feeling bruised. Joe's lack of commercial grounding had been brutally exposed, John's name had been tarnished, and Christine's last salary cheque had bounced. And for years afterwards, John found himself soothing and helping disgruntled customers.

"I think they thought it was going to be easy and glamorous," Christine sighs. "But John had built himself a reputation by doing what he said he was going to do."

Joe is no longer directly involved in classic cars, nor does he race, but after six fruitful years with the sales department at Bristol Audi, he has gone on to develop a motor trade niche of his own and now runs a successful business as a wholesale trader in prestige cars. He is philosophical about the early years of his career: he could have handled things better, as could his dad, but he has far more good memories than bad. Would he have swapped the travel, the racing, the excitement, for the further education and professional ladder-climbing of so many of his contemporaries? Joe's answer is unequivocal. "Not for a moment."

There are no prizes for guessing who supplied the grunty hunkered-down E320 CDI Mercedes diesel estate which John currently uses as his everyday transport – for customers, Healey engines, sets of wheels, and whatever else needs to get to and from the farm. "It's not perfect," Joe told his father when he first showed it him, "but then, by the time you've finished with it, it'll be completely knackered!"

A lot of fences have been mended in the intervening ten years. "Joe and I have a good relationship now," assures Christine, "in fact I was in San Carlos a couple of months ago and Joe was there with some colleagues. He said, 'if it wasn't for this lady, I wouldn't do my accounts as well as I do because she was always on my back – to fill in the cheque stub, to put the cheque number on the invoices ... ' and in front of everyone he said, 'thank you for that.' That made me feel really proud because I started working for John when Joe was a teenager. There were times when I almost felt like a second mum to the boys."

The boys, indeed the whole family, would soon need all the support they could get, because the Chatham world

was shattered in November 2000 when John suffered a serious stroke. Vicky takes up the story.

"It was particularly frightening for Oliver and Jack, who were both too young to know what strokes did to people. Overnight they saw this big strong man turn into someone who couldn't walk and could barely speak. John was a week in hospital, but even when he came home I had to cut up his food for him and he couldn't move around much.

"John had his stroke only two months after I returned to flying with BA in Bristol, at the age of 50. But the company were great, they said, 'don't worry, your job's here.'"

It was just as well that her employer was understanding because although family and friends did what they could – particularly Vicky's parents and Charlotte – it was Vicky who had to hold everything together. She remembers these weeks as the most stressful time of her entire life. "The phone never stopped ringing and there was an endless stream of visitors. I had a teenager and a child to look after, a big house, a business and a new job – and flying full-time at the age of 50 is gruelling – plus a husband recovering from a major stroke. I probably didn't realize at the time how depressed John was. He didn't know how well he would recover, and whether he would have another stroke, but I didn't have time to take much of that on board. I was so pleased when someone finally asked how I was getting on!"

John made a good, albeit incomplete, recovery. His mind is 100 per cent, but he walks with a shuffling gait and his speech is slurred, so he sounds like he's leaving the pub

Performance engineer Dan Howell with GRX in 2009.

before he's even arrived – his friends call him 'The Hallen Mumbler.' Getting in and out of Healeys is much harder than it used to be and competition driving is definitely off the agenda (though in 2009 he couldn't resist entertaining the Silverstone paddock with a few doughnuts in his E-Type). But there have been no major health problems since and he is able to lead a pretty normal life, so he counts himself lucky.

It was nearly six months before John could take the reins of the business again, six months when scarcely a day went by without a visit from one medical professional or another. Today a physiotherapist, tomorrow a speech therapist, next day an occupational therapist. But together they got the Hallen Mumbler back into the driving seat.

In the meantime, Dan Howell did a sterling job keeping the business ticking over, the most important task being to complete the first Healey 3000S. Dan has since joined the payroll full-time as performance engineer. The rest of the team are all freelances: trimmer, Pete Cagna; bodyman, Dominic Graffagnino; bookkeeper, Christine Maxwell and engine builder, Nick Pride.

The 3000S, incidentally, is a purely Chatham creation, intended to echo the 100S which competed at Sebring. In DD 300, John did of course have an original Sebring Healey 3000, but unlike the four-cylinder car, the factory never marketed a replica. The 3000S is John's attempt to put that right and is based on the MkII chassis with a centre-change gearbox. The engine features an 'exciting' camshaft and a six-branch exhaust, plus triple SU carburettors, the latter chosen to provide a good compromise between power and usability. "In period they raced with two or three SUs, or triple Webers," John explains. The package is finished off with British Racing Green paint, red leather, S-type bonnet catches and S-type seats, making for "a nice usable road/rally car." To date he has built three, of which the first went to William Cadbury from the confectionery family.

Currently, neither Oliver nor Jack is involved in the business, but both are committed petrolheads.

Oliver Chatham's first taste of car control came before he was able to walk. Left alone momentarily in an XJ6, he yanked the lever out of park and happily rolled off the drive. Then when he was about four, he set about building his own car, from whatever bits he could find laying around the numerous garages and stores that are scattered about the farm. His parents discovered him sat in it, fantasizing about being a racing driver. Shortly after this he found his way into a real car, started the engine and revved it until a fan blade tried to make its way through the bonnet.

At the time of writing, Oliver and John are amusing themselves developing a hot Chevette for classic rallying. With 250bhp and little more than a shell and roll-cage to haul around, it is very quick and is already bringing a smile to both their faces. However, motorsport is strictly a hobby for Oliver, who has gone to drama school and is intent on

Engine builder Nick Pride.

Child labour: Oliver's first job – "sand this door."

Five boys with five toys in 1995: left to right, Joe Senior, Oliver, John, Jack and Joe Junior.

making the entertainment business his career. In this, to Vicky's surprise, he is following in his mother's footsteps – between the ages of 7 and 17, she did a lot of acting, on TV, film and stage.

Jack's enthusiasm developed later than Oliver's and for a long time he showed little interest in cars. "After we came here," Vicky recalls, "I'd sometimes see him sitting bored on the settee and say, 'there's this lovely garage outside, why don't you make use of it, aren't you interested?' And he'd say, 'no.'"

But the acquisition of a driving licence changed Jack's

attitude completely and John, sensing his youngest son's passion awakening, gave him a rebuild project – a recently reacquired MGC roadster, which he had converted to V8 power in the 1970s. "Now you can't stop him," says Vicky. At the time of writing the C is well advanced, with huge blistered wheel arches, a pristine paint job (the same green as VHY 5H, complete with yellow nose) and a hot Rover V8 almost ready to be dropped in.

In the longer term, Jack has talked about joining his father in the business, which has expanded considerably since its tentative rebirth following the move from Egerton

Holland 2001: John with Oliver at his first competitive event.

Jack learning to race at Castle Combe.

Road. It won't happen soon – John and Vicky are encouraging Jack to gain the grounding that Joe never had, by working elsewhere and getting formal business training. He has already completed a race technician's course at Silverstone and is hoping to gain experience with a NASCAR team in the US. It remains to be seen whether John Chatham Cars eventually becomes John Chatham & Son, but John would certainly be delighted if it did.

It was fortunate for John that by the time he had the stroke his competitive career was already petering out. To have been yanked out of the four-point harness in his prime would have been unbearable.

After the stroke, John contented himself with letting others drive his cars and enjoying the spectacle. Indeed he still does. In 2009, GRX, which had been dormant for a while, emerged from rebuild in rally trim and was raced by Oliver in the John Gott Memorial Trophy at Silverstone. And his co-driver? None other than Steve Bicknell.

For a while, John continued to exercise DD in the same way. Apart from the Jack Sears drive mentioned earlier, Chris Clarkson had a number of outings in the car in the five years after John's illness, including a big win at Thruxton in 2002, in partnership with Whizzo Williams in the all comers race at the 50th anniversary Healey meeting. They qualified seventh, but Whizzo came through to the front after torrential rain depleted the top runners.

Eventually though, John decided that he could no longer do justice to the old warrior that had been in his hands almost continuously for over 40 years. It was one of the highest mileage racing cars anywhere, having competed all over Britain, in America and at many prestigious Continental circuits including Spa, Dijon, Montlhéry and Nürburgring (though never at Monza, that honour fell to GRX). Now it needed a new home. He sold it to Karsten Le Blank and Christiaen van Lanschot for around £250,000 in 2005.

It was, fittingly, two Bristolians who gave DD its last ever outing at Castle Combe in John's ownership, when Julian Bronson partnered Chris Clarkson at the 2005 Easter Monday meeting. And it was Chris again who had the last drive of all, at Goodwood the same year, when he beat the Le Mans Morgan Plus 4 Supersport, TOK 258, to win the Fordwater Trophy race. This was particularly satisfying, as DD and TOK were perennial rivals and had tussled many times over the years.

Does he miss the racing? "Not really," he says, "I've done it. I competed in 21 countries over 40 years. Nothing is for ever. I said I'd never sell DD, but when it went, it wasn't really the wrench everybody thought it would be. It had served its purpose. It was time it moved on for somebody else to enjoy."

Jack in front of Wellinghouse Farm with a karting trophy and an old Minardi F1 suit.

John Chatham and John Lewis with their Modsports mounts. This photo was taken in the pit lane at the 2005 BRDC Silverstone track day – the first time for many years that both Johns and both cars had been together. (© Mike Jiggle).

Wizzo in action at Thruxton in 2002 when he and Chris Clarkson took DD to a win in terrible conditions. (© Steve Jones)

Vicky adds: "You have to be realistic. There are people out there still racing in their 70s and 80s, like Ted Williams and Stirling Moss, but even if John hadn't had the stroke, he may not have been in a position to do it financially. The business is a good substitute, it keeps John involved and maybe Jack will start competing ... "

Drive into Wellinghouse Farm today and you will probably find John looking much as he always has – beard, glasses, grin, grubby clothes – and doing what he always has – working on Healeys, joking with customers and avoiding paperwork if at all possible. And as the business is busier than ever, despite not advertising or having a

Chris Clarkson (left) and David Smithies with DD 300 after taking it to a win in the Fordwater Trophy race at the 2005 Goodwood Revival. (© Peter Dzwig)

John Chatham and family, October 2009: (left to right, back row) daughter Charlotte and partner Steve, son Jack, son Oliver, John, son Joe and partner Emma with their children Lucy and James; (front row) Charlotte's children Ruby and Charlie, and wife Vicky.

website, the customers must like it that way.

John is the first to admit that he is now working to higher standards than ever before. In part, this is because techniques and materials have improved, and because he is still learning, but mostly it's because the customers can now afford to have the job done properly.

"It's only since I've been out of the garage business altogether and have 'retired' that I've really enjoyed dealing with customers. Now that Healeys are classic cars and are no longer something which people drive every day, there's no great demand for them to be ready for a particular day. People want them readied for racing, or rallying, or as a road car, and these guys have got the money to spend on them. They enjoy the cars and I enjoy making them right for them. So here I am living in this old rambling place, surrounded by Healeys, doing what I like to do. And I wouldn't want to stop."

DD 300:
A BRIEF HISTORY

- Originally registered UJB 143, one of four British Racing Green factory racers built in 1959, of which three competed at the 1960 Sebring 12 Hours. Driven by Jack Sears and Peter Riley, third in class.

- Subsequently competed at Le Mans 24 Hours in 1960, again with Sears and Riley. Retired.

- Bought from the factory in late 1960 by David Dixon and re-registered DD 300. Privately entered for Le Mans 1961, driven by Dickie Stoop and John Bekaert. Retired. Raced by Pat Moss at the Brands Hatch Boxing Day meeting, 1961.

- Entered for 1962 Le Mans, driven by Bob Olthoff and John Whitmore. Retired after 18 hours while running tenth.

- Placed second in 1962 Rand 9 Hours in the hands of Bob Olthoff.

- Sold to Robbie Gordon in 1963, driven by Peter Jackson.

- Badly damaged at Snetterton by Julian Hasler.

- Bought by John Chatham in 1964 and rebuilt to compete in GT category, initially painted Sebring Blue and with standard wheels.

- Repainted red in winter 1966-67 and fitted with 8½in wide wheels to compete in Modsports.

- Fitted with 10½in wide wheels part-way through 1967 season, class win in Fred W Dixon Marque Car Championship that year.

- Dominated Modsports racing during 1968-69, notching up a record number of race wins in 1968.

- Sold to David Weir in 1970, briefly raced by him. Also raced by Alain de Cadenet.

- Reacquired in 1971 by John Chatham and restored to original profile to race in the Thoroughbred Series, painted metallic green. Fitted with steel wheels early 1971, Minilites 1971-72, thereafter wires. Won the series in 1972.

- Raced in classic events throughout Europe all through the 1970s, '80s and '90s, driven by Gerry Marshall, Stirling Moss and others in addition to John Chatham. Repainted British Racing Green in late 1980s.

- Overall victory in the 1990 Conclave Challenge series in the USA.

- Reunited with Jack Sears at the Austin-Healey International in Switzerland, 2004.

- Sold in 2005 to Karsten Le Blank and Christiaen van Lanschot. Probably one of the highest-mileage racing cars anywhere.

DD 300 in its original form, seen here being driven by Pat Moss at the 1961 Boxing Day Brands Hatch meeting. (© Ted Walker)

DD 300 as it is today. This photo was taken on the lawn at Wellinghouse Farm, not long before the car was sold.

John David Chatham: 40 Years of Highs and Lows

II

A SUMMARY OF HIS SPORTING CAREER

1960-63

Acquired A-H 100/4 BN1, SAL 75, 1960. First ever competitive event in 1960, sprint at Church Lawton. Shortly afterwards entered sprint at Hullavington, nearly rolled the car. Followed by entries in races, rallies, sprints, hillclimbs, trials, and autocrosses, all over the UK. Numerous class and outright wins. Joined White Horse Motor Club 1960, Austin-Healey Club 1961 (inaugural committee member of SW Centre) and also member of Bristol Motorcycle & Light Car Club.

1963-1964

Acquired A-H 100/4 BN1, DGL 666, 1963. Entries in trials and autocrosses nationwide, including Exeter, Lands End, and Derbyshire. Various class and outright wins. Continued to campaign SAL 75 on the circuits.

1964-67

Acquired A-H 3000 MkI BN7, DD 300, 1964. Car purchased badly damaged and rebuilt to compete in GT category. First race after rebuild 1965. Numerous races in 1966 and 1967. Class win in Fred W Dixon Marque Car Championship 1967. Continued to campaign DGL 666 in off-road events.

1968

DD 300 developed steadily and raced intensively. Class win in Modsports Championship, following 28 race wins and class lap records at ten circuits. Front cover of *Autosport* magazine, 21 February 1969. Accident at Silverstone, and an even more serious accident at Mallory Park.

John in 1967.

1969

DD 300 raced intensively. Won class in Modsports Championship.

1969-70

Acquired MGC GT Sebring, VHY 5H, in parts, 1969. Entered 1970 Targa Florio with Alan Harvey. Finished 39th out of 90 starters, suffered misfire initially and brake failure latterly.

1970
Drove Porsche 906 with Mike Coombe in Vila Real GP. Finished race, but disqualified for helmet infringement.

1971
Entered Porsche 911S in GT class at Le Mans, with Mike Coombe and Willie Tuckett. Failed to qualify.

1971
DD 300 re-emerges in John's hands, rebuilt to original spec for historic racing.

1971-1999
Entries and wins with DD 300 in numerous historic races throughout UK, highlights blow. Continental events include Coupe de l'Age d'Or at Montlhéry (1970s, 1983-87, 1992-93, 1995), the Six Hours at Spa, plus races at Nürburgring, Zandvoort and Le Mans Bugatti. Also guest drives in wide variety of machinery.

1971
First overall in DD 300 at Coupe de l'Age d'Or, Montlhéry. (Year uncertain).

1972
Won Thoroughbred Series in DD 300.

1972-73
Campaigned MGC GT Sebring Lightweight in Modsports, built from parts acquired in 1969. Took 3-litre lap record at Silverstone, otherwise modest success.

1974-1999
Rallied A-H 3000 MkIII BJ8, GRX 884D. Entries in numerous historic rallies in UK and abroad. Still in John's ownership. Highlights below.

1983
Entered GRX 884D in Coronation Rally, August 1983, co-driver Phil Saddington. Serious accident, car badly damaged after rolling end over end.

1984
Second overall and first in class in DD 300 at Coupe de l'Age d'Or, Montlhéry.

1987
Partnered Nick Howell in Coppa d'Italia in A-H 3000 MkII, 67 ARX, unplaced.

1987
In DD 300, won Big Healey race at Grand Prix de l'Age d'Or, Montlhéry.

1988
Placed second in Pirelli Marathon in GRX 884D.

1989
Entered GRX 884D in Marathon, started 75, leading by third day, then retired due to accident.

1989
Entered GRX 884 in Viking Rally in Norway, with Anne Hall. Won Ladies Cup.

1989
Partnered Beppi Bertipaglia in his A-H 3000 MkI for Targa Florio Storica. Spun on oil spill and retired with body and mechanical damage.

1990
In DD 300, led winning UK team in Conclave Challenge, five-race A-H international series in US.

1991
Entered A-H 100S BN1, OYY 210 (built from damaged car acquired approximately 1969) in Pirelli Marathon. Retired with clutch failure.

1991
Entered OYY 210 in International Rally Britannia, rolled car at Donington Park, but completed event.

1991
Drove DD 300 at Nürburgring in Eiffel Classic, later in same meeting partnered Mark Schmidt in A-H 3000 MkI in appalling conditions, retired for safety reasons.

1992
Entered two cars in Carrera Panamericana: drove OYY 210 with Trevor Seckel (retired with engine failure while leading class) and Jeremy Barras' Healey 100/4 for Joe Chatham/Jeremy Barras (won class). Barras car fitted for this event with diesel-block engine jointly developed by John Chatham and Geoff Healey.

1993
Only single-seat drive, swapped DD 300 for Ted Williams' ex-Ronnie Peterson March 711 for a race at Zandvoort Noisy Weekend, organized by the Austin-Healey Owners Club Nederland (Holland) in August 1993.

1995
Entered GRX 884D in London-Mexico, with Steve Bicknell. Retired with engine failure in Peru.

1996
Partnered Robert Shaw and Ted Worswick in 56 FBC at Spa Six Hours. Retired with electrical problem.

1996
Entered GRX 884D in Coys International classic meet at Silverstone. Made top-ten run off.

1998
Guest drive at Donald Healey commemorative race at Bathurst 1000 meeting, Australia.

1999
Austin-Healey Club international week based in Luxembourg, competed in various events including a regularity rally in GRX 884D with Anne Hall – placed first.

2000
Retired from competition driving.

瓦

John Chatham can be reached at:
Wellinghouse Farm, Moorhouse Lane, Hallen, Bristol BS10 7RT, UK.
Tel +44(0)1179 501836.
Mobile +44 (0)7785 502141.

This Doug Eyre cartoon is one of a series depicting motorsport characters, produced for Vauxhall Sport as part of the company's support for the 16 October 1994 round of the Touring Car World Cup. (© Doug Eyre)

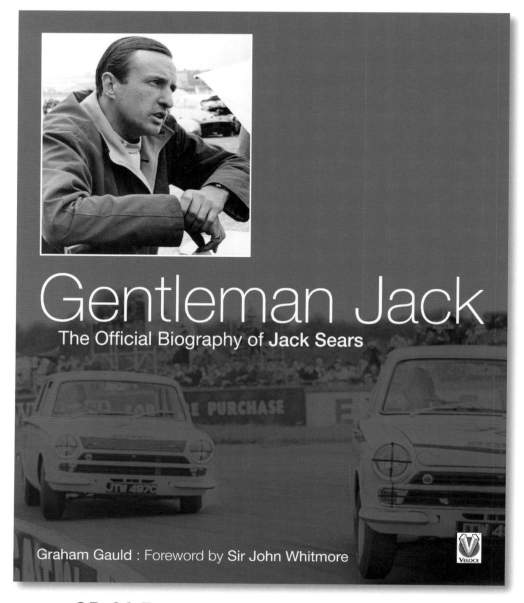

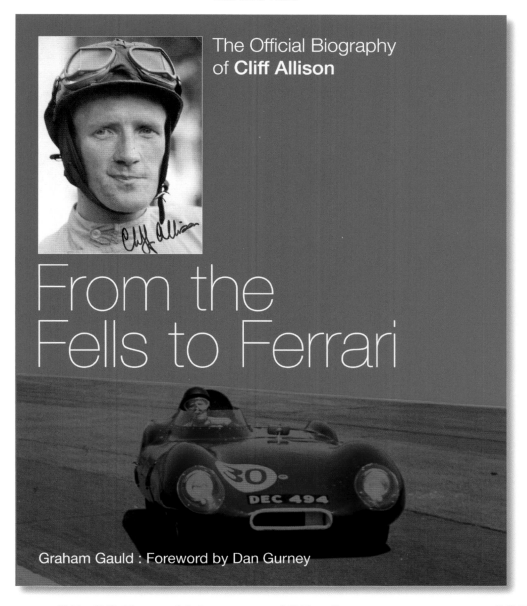

INDEX